FAITH
ROOTS

Learning from and Sharing
Witness with Jewish People

FAITH ROOTS

Learning from and Sharing Witness with Jewish People

James R. Leaman

Evangel Press

2000 Evangel Way
Nappanee, Indiana 46550-0189

Faith Roots, by James R. Leaman. © 1993 by Evangel Publishing House. All rights reserved. No part of this book may be reproduced in any form or by any process or technique without written permission, except in case of brief quotations in critical articles or reviews. For information, write to Evangel Publishing House, 2000 Evangel Way, P.O. Box 189, Nappanee IN 46550.

Cover design: Tracey Owen

Cover photo: A giant menorah, symbol of the State of Israel, stands in front of the Knesset, Israel's parliament. Compliments of The Israel Ministry of Tourism, North America.

Library of Congress Catalog Number: 92-075500
ISBN: 0-916035-57-3

Printed in the United States of America

5 4 3 2

Dedicated
to my parents
Ivan D. and Ethel M. (d. 1988) Leaman
who modeled for me
lives of faithful, godly witness

Contents

Introduction

Since the reemergence of Israel as a national entity, Paul's picture of the Jewish people being grafted back into the olive tree as a whole ("all Israel") has been underscored. Paul's ultimate hope of course is not for national restoration but national salvation. But a national regathering does seem to be anticipated in Scripture, and it is difficult to conceive of any large-scale awakening among the Jewish people to the truth of Jesus as Messiah, apart from that logistical condition.

However, the physical regathering of Israel is not the only contemporary event giving credence to Paul's hope. A second is the reemergence of the Messianic Jewish movement. Originally Christianity was Jewish. The early disciples in Jerusalem were devout, practicing Jews. They attended temple services. They kept the Law. But they also boldly proclaimed Jesus, crucified by humanity but raised by the Father, as the long-awaited Messiah.

James Leaman's *Faith Roots* affirms these beginnings and calls contemporary believers to be faithful in reminding our Jewish friends of this heritage and of their need today, and ours, to repent and embrace Jesus (Yeshua) as the Messiah. He affirms that God has a special place in his heart for the people he chose to be "a light to the nations," that "to the Jew first" is not merely a statement of chronology but a strong affirmation of the importance of loving our Jewish neighbors, and that to do so is inevitably to enrich our own spiritual walk by reminding us of the Jewish roots of our faith. The Christian faith must be shared with all regardless of national background, race, sex, or any potential smoke screen to our common humanity. And the Jewish people are included—not to be neglected—in this obligation. This is especially true in light of the unique place the Jewish people have had in God's plan in history—past, present, and future.

Art McPhee
Pastor, Good Shepherd Christian Fellowship
Needham Heights, Massachusetts

Acknowledgements

There have been many encouragers and enablers in this book project, and I want to say "Thank you!" to them. Unfortunately I cannot name everyone.

First, I thank my wife Beth for the faithful encourager she has been to me for the last twenty-three years and specifically for her support during this writing project. I appreciate the support of my children Tim and Maria. Maria, a student at Lancaster Mennonite High School, provided the illustrations on page 117.

Second, there are several persons whom I consider as especially significant in nurturing within me a vision for the importance of the gospel message of Messiah being shared with Messiah's own Jewish people:

—Ruth Graybill, retired but still active in sharing a witness with Jewish people, and a member of the congregation I pastor;

—Luke Stoltzfus, my overseer in Philadelphia, who has had a long-time interest in promoting a Christian witness among Jewish people;

—David Shenk, presently Director of Overseas Ministries of Eastern Mennonite Board of Missions and Charities (EMBMC), who personally encouraged Beth and me to attend the 1986 Lausanne Consultation for Jewish Evangelism Conference held in England;

—Philip Bottomley, friend and seminar teacher (formerly director of A Christian Ministry Among Jewish People—CMJ/USA), who mentored me by his teaching and introduction to helpful books. His seminar, *How to Introduce Your Jewish Friends to Jesus*, was especially instructive.

Third, I acknowledge several groups of encouragers:

—the Shofar Committee of the Home Ministries Department of EMBMC, who sponsored this writing project;

—the early editorial committee for this project: Freeman Miller, chairperson of EMBMC's Shofar Committee when I began writing; Rich Nichol, Messianic pastor; and Art McPhee, pastor and author;

—the Shofar Committee support group: Paul Dagen, Luke Stoltzfus, Pauline Stoltzfus, and John Nissley (John has been a wonderful personal encourager in this project.);

—an Oxford Circle Mennonite Church (where I pastor) adult Sunday school class who used the early material of this project as a Sunday school elective which I taught;

—my colleagues in JOPPA (Jewish Outreach Partnership in the Philadelphia Area);

—friends of the Shofar Committee who gave support in prayer and in contributions to subsidize publication.

Fourth, I thank those who helped with technical assistance and expertise:

—Kathy Farrel of EMBMC Home Ministries Department who kindly labored to type my first handwritten drafts into the word processor/computer;

—June Burkholder, who later patiently guided me in learning to use a word processor, as well as did editing and printing out on the word processor;

—Otto Schlack, who made a word processor available for my use;

—Janet Kreider, as editor of EMBMC's *Missionary Messenger*, who printed segments of this manuscript and provided valuable editorial assistance in the process;

—Nancy Witmer, a free-lance writer, who gave helpful counsel and made good suggestions for changes in the manuscript;

—to the staff of Evangel Publishing House: Executive Director Roger Lloyd Williams, General Editor Glen Pierce, Project Editor Helen Johns, and others who brought this writing project and vision to fruition and reality in its publication—my heartfelt gratitude and appreciation.

May this book be one small means of helping to spread the message of Messiah, especially to Messiah's own people. To God be the glory!

James R. Leaman

1

The Motivation

Questions

Fred and Kristi observed their new neighbors with curiosity. Every Saturday morning, Mr. Goldberg and his two sons, dressed in suits and wearing little caps, went away together for several hours. In mid-October, they built a plywood shelter in the yard outside their back door.

"I thought our neighbors were building a tool shed," Fred said one evening as he and Kristi were finishing dinner. "But it looks like a temporary structure, and it has an open top."

The next day, Kristi watched as Mrs. Goldberg and her daughter decorated the shelter with grapevines and colorful gourds. Mr. Goldberg laid dried cornstalks and leafy branches across the open roof.

"Kristi, do you know what the Goldbergs are building in their backyard?" Mrs. Holland, another neighbor, looked as if she would burst with her knowledge. "They're Jewish, and that shelter has something to do with a Jewish fall festival." She thought for a minute. "I can't remember the name of it. The Goldbergs aren't the only Jewish family in our community," Mrs. Holland continued. "Several young families have moved here recently from New York City. On Saturday mornings the men and boys and a few women meet in one of their homes in a basement that has been renovated into a small synagogue."

Kristi was quiet as Mrs. Holland spoke. How did this woman always know what was happening, she wondered.

"I don't like Jewish families moving into our community," Mrs. Holland said. "They're not Christian, and wasn't it the Jews who crucified Jesus?" She shrugged her shoulders. "I guess there's not much we can do about it though."

Later, Kristi told her husband about the conversation.

"I don't like Mrs. Holland's attitude toward people who are different from her," Fred said. "We try to respect others. Maybe there's some way we can share our faith with the Goldbergs."

"I'm not sure I know how to share our Christian faith with Jewish people," Kristi asked. "The Goldbergs are very religious, and they certainly appear quite happy. If they're already worshiping God, I wonder whether they even need to know about Jesus?"

Fred discussed these questions with his brother, a college religion professor.

"Jewish people have all they need to know about approaching God in their Hebrew Bible," his brother said. "Jesus is for Gentiles. Besides, Christians have a history of persecuting and killing Jewish people. It would be an insult to ask them to believe in Jesus."

"I'm not sure that I agree with my brother," Fred said later. "Jesus was Jewish. If Jesus was for everyone, that would include Jewish people, wouldn't it?"

"Let's talk to our pastor about it," Kristi said. "In the meantime, let's get acquainted with the Goldbergs. Maybe they'll tell us about their backyard shelter and the fall celebration that goes with it."

Motivations for witnessing to Jewish people

Is it appropriate to share about Messiah Jesus with Jewish friends and neighbors? Here are some responses to that question:

1. The church owes a debt of gratitude to the Jewish people. Jesus said, "Salvation is from the Jews" (John 4:22). God chose to provide, through the Jewish people, salvation and a Savior for all people of the world who respond to him. A response of eternal thanksgiving is to share that message of salvation with Jewish people.

2. God promises to bless those who bless his chosen people.

> The Lord had said to Abram, "Leave your country, your people and your father's household and go to the land I will show you. I will make you into a great nation and I will bless you; I will make your name great, and you will be a blessing. I will bless those who bless you, and whoever curses you I will curse; and all peoples on earth will be blessed through you." (Genesis 12:1-3)

Sharing the good news of Messiah Jesus with Jewish people is certainly one important way of blessing them. When we do that, we can expect to receive God's blessing in return.

A senior church statesman worked for much of his life with a mission board that has experienced God's blessing. He believed that part of the reason for the board's fruitful ministry is that it has been involved in promoting a witness among Jewish people.

3. Israel is God's missionary people, supremely through Messiah.

> He said to me, "You are my servant, Israel, in whom I will display my splendor.". . . He says: "It is too small a thing for you to be my servant to restore the tribes of Jacob and bring back those of Israel I have kept. I will also make you a light for the Gentiles, that you may bring my salvation to the ends of the earth." (Isaiah 49:3, 6)

God chose Israel to be his light to the world. Salvation has come to the Gentiles through the Jewish people. *Messianic Jews* (See Glossary, p. 165) will enlarge the evangelistic thrust of the Christian Church.

4. The gospel is to the Jew first.

> I am not ashamed of the gospel, because it is the power of God for the salvation of everyone who believes: first for the Jew, then for the Gentile. (Romans 1:16)

Jesus went first and primarily to his own Jewish people. Paul, although called to be a missionary to the Gentiles, also went first to the synagogue when he entered a new city.

Hudson Taylor, pioneer missionary to China, sent an offering back to England each January to help support a missionary society working with Jewish people. On his check, he wrote, "To the Jew first." It was his way of following the principle of Romans 1:16.

5. The salvation of Jewish people will greatly enrich God's kingdom. Missionary Paul wrote:

> Again, I ask: Did they [the Jews] stumble so as to fall beyond recovery? Not at all! Rather, because of their transgression, salvation has come to the Gentiles to make Israel envious. But if their transgression means riches for the world, and their loss means riches for the Gentiles, how much greater riches will their fullness bring! I am talking to you Gentiles. Inasmuch as I am the apostle to the Gentiles, I make much of my ministry in the hope that I may somehow arouse my own people to envy and save some of them. For if their rejection is the reconciliation of the world, what will their acceptance be but life from the dead? If the part of the dough offered as firstfruits is holy, then the whole batch is holy; if the root is holy, so are the branches. (Romans 11:11-16)

God has not rejected Israel as a people. He has preserved the Jewish people through thousands of years of persecution. These verses from Romans 11 indicate that God still has kingdom work to be done through the Jewish people. Some propose that as it goes with the Jewish people—in terms of their attitude in accepting Jesus as Messiah, so it goes with the rest of the world—in terms of world redemption. (See Acts 3:19-21.)

Objections raised

Some Christians, however, believe Jews do not need a witness about Jesus. They believe Jewish people have all they need for salvation in the First Covenant[1] made with them by God through Abraham, Moses, and David. These people believe God has already shown the Jewish people how they can relate to him and that it would be arrogant of Christians to tell them they need something more.

Other Christians say it would be an insult to tell Jews that Jesus is their Savior, because millions of them have been persecuted and killed by people professing to follow Jesus. A third objection to witnessing to Jewish people is that it is a difficult task with little fruit. Some would argue that it is better to invest missionary personnel and dollars into Latin America or Africa or Asia where one might expect more results.

Do Jewish people need Jesus?

What does the Bible say? Let's look first at the Hebrew Scriptures (Old Testament).[2] Jewish people[3] are the descendants of Abraham through his son Isaac. (See Genesis 17:15-19.) God chose to especially reveal himself to the family of Abraham, the people of Israel (the name given to Isaac's son Jacob—Genesis 32:28).

Through Israel, God wanted to reach all peoples, the Gentiles[4] also. In his first promise to Abram (later called Abraham),[5] God said, "All peoples on earth will be

---

1 "First Covenant" is positive terminology for "Old Covenant."

2 "Hebrew Scriptures" is a more positive term than "Old Testament." One could also use "Tenach," the Hebrew term for what Christians call the "Old Testament."

3 The name "Jew" comes from Isaac's grandson Judah (one of Jacob's twelve sons and one of the twelve tribes of Israel).

4 The term "Gentile" comes from the Hebrew word *Goyim*, meaning "nations."

5 Abram means "exalted father" and Abraham "father of many." (See Genesis 17:5.)

blessed through you." In Isaiah 66:19, God referred to Jewish people who would ". . . proclaim my glory among the nations."

God did, however, particularly reach out to the Jewish nation. The nation was small in number, but God chose to commit himself to this insignificant people and make them significant by blessing them with his presence and love. (See Deuteronomy 7:7-9.) If God chose to especially reach out to this particular people, should we have any problem with focusing on a witness to Jewish people?

God continued to focus on a ministry to Jews even through his son, Messiah Jesus. Although Jesus touched the lives of a Syrian-Phoenician-Greek woman, a Roman centurion, and a Samaritan woman and her townspeople, he primarily ministered among his own Jewish people. Matthew 10:5-6 says that Jesus sent out the twelve disciples with these instructions, "Do not go among the Gentiles or enter any town of the Samaritans. Go rather to the lost sheep of Israel." The people of Israel were the central focus of Jesus' ministry.

The testimony of the Gospels is that Jesus came to save *his own Jewish people*, and also the rest of the world, whoever believes in him. The First Covenant looked forward to fulfillment in Messiah and the New Covenant. Jesus came to fulfill the Law, the Psalms, and the Prophets of the original covenant, "to fill them full" with meaning. To pretend that Jews do not need to hear about Jesus would be to ignore the Scriptures and to do a disservice to Jewish people. Consider these Scriptures:

> Jesus answered, "I am the way and the truth and the life. No one comes to the Father except through me." (John 14:6)

> For God so loved the world that he gave his one and only Son, that whoever believes in him shall not perish but have eternal life. (John 3:16)

The story of the book of Acts is first a story of God's pouring out his Holy Spirit upon godly *Jewish* men and women gathered in unity and prayer. When the Spirit came upon them, they witnessed boldly about Jesus. The 3,000 who responded to Peter's message that Pentecost day and the many who responded as reported in Acts 4:4 and 6:7 (including a large number of priests) were Jewish people. The outreach of that early, Apostolic, Jewish "church" was first to other Jews. God did intervene to call those early believers in Messiah to evangelize Gentiles also. Peter was converted in his thinking, and God directed him to preach to the Roman centurion Cornelius and his household. Even before that, Saul had been dramatically turned around by God and called to carry the name of Yeshua (Hebrew for Jesus) to Gentiles and their kings as well as to the people of Israel. (See Acts 9:15.) The church in Antioch was a cross-cultural fellowship. (See Acts 11:19-26 and 13:1-3.) The Jerusalem conference focused on how to incorporate Gentile believers into the family of God which had been Jewish up to that time.

Nonetheless, as Paul (the transformed Saul) went out on his missionary ventures, he routinely found his way first to the local synagogue to present the good news of Messiah Jesus.

> When they had passed through Amphipolis and Apollonia, they came to Thessalonica, where there was a Jewish synagogue. As his custom was, Paul went into the synagogue, and on three Sabbath days he reasoned with them from the Scriptures, explaining and proving that the Christ had to suffer and rise from the dead. "This Jesus I am proclaiming to you is the Christ," he said. Some of the Jews were persuaded and joined Paul and Silas, as did a large number of God-fearing Greeks and not a few prominent women. (Acts 17:1-4)

According to the New Testament pattern, the Jewish people are to be included in the Great Commission of Jesus—to proclaim the gospel and make disciples of all nations. Paul proclaimed and modeled a priority in witnessing to Jewish people. Note again Romans 1:16:

> I am not ashamed of the gospel, because it is the power of God for the salvation of everyone who believes: first for the Jew, then for the Gentile.

At the 1986 Third International Lausanne Consultation on Jewish Evangelism, convened in England, Mitch Glaser, a Messianic Jew, addressed the topic, "To the Jew First." Glaser suggested that "first" means "above all, especially," the gospel is for the Jew. He noted the similar meaning of "first" in Matthew 6:33, ". . . seek first his kingdom" (seek "above all" his kingdom).

Glaser asserted that we need not be reluctant about giving special focus to Jewish people in outreach, because God himself especially chose Jewish people in salvation history. He urged the church to do world missions as well.

> Salvation is found in no one else [except Jesus], for there is no other name under heaven given to men by which we must be saved. (Acts 4:12)

> He who has the Son has life; he who does not have the Son of God does not have life. (1 John 5:12)

These texts (along with John 14:6 quoted earlier) state that only through Jesus can anyone find salvation (deliverance from the power of sin and evil, entrance into a new life of shalom and forgiveness, and belonging to the community of God and his people now and forever).

We know that godly Jewish men and women of the First Covenant era found salvation as they encountered God by faith through obedience to the Law, offering the sacrifices, and worshiping God. Yet this salvation anticipated the One who was yet to come, Messiah, who would be the supreme sacrifice for sin.

At the 1986 Lausanne Conference, Anglican Bishop John Taylor of the St. Albans Church, England, addressed the theme, "There Is Only One Name of Salvation" (from Acts 4:12). In this context, Peter and John were being questioned about how the crippled man at the Gate Beautiful had been healed. They turned their interrogation into a proclamation of the gospel. Peter declared the man had been healed by the name of Jesus Christ of Nazareth. This is the first Scripture that places "Jesus of Nazareth," (a common reference in the Gospels) side by side with "Christ" (Messiah). Peter was announcing that Jesus of Nazareth was Messiah, as he quoted from a Messianic passage in Psalm 118 about the rejected stone becoming the capstone. It was the power of Messiah which healed this man, Peter proclaimed, and, he went on to say, it is only in the name of Jesus Christ of Nazareth that there is salvation.

A "two-covenant" theology is unacceptable! Such a theology, which some Christian scholars propose, says that Jews can find salvation through the First Covenant of God with Abraham, Moses, and David, and that Gentiles can find salvation through the New Covenant of God in Jesus. But Paul declared, in Romans 1:16, that the gospel is the power of God for salvation for everyone who believes, for the Jew and for the Gentile. And that gospel, he wrote in the fourth verse of Romans 1, is the good news of Jesus Christ our Lord.

Does a history of anti-Semitism nullify a witness to Jewish people?

There is a horrible history of Christians torturing and murdering Jews in the Crusades, the Spanish Inquisition, Russian pogroms, and the German Nazi Holocaust. But we cannot let that keep us from witnessing for Jesus to Jewish people. We must repudiate these sins of the past and confess our own sins of prejudice. We can in humility share the reality of the love of God through his Son Jesus. God himself suffered in the torturous, humiliating death of his son.

Some have protested that it would be anti-Semitic (anti-Jewish) to desire for Jews to be evangelized with the gospel of Jesus. One theologian has said that if Jews said "yes" to Jesus, there would be no more Jews—that Hitler's goal would be accomplished. However, at the 1986 Lausanne Consultation, Gerald Anderson of the Overseas Ministries Study Center commented that many Jewish believers in Jesus embrace their Jewishness more so than they did prior to believing in Messiah. My seminary Hebrew professor asserted that *not* to witness to Jewish people would be anti-Semitic, because that would exclude them from opportunities to respond to the gospel of Messiah Jesus.

Is a witness to Jewish people too difficult?

It is God's responsibility to bring people to himself and transform them. The *gospel is the power of God* for salvation. Our responsibility is to share a clear presentation of the good news and to be available to be used by God.

Many Jews have responded and are responding to the gospel. Even though it may seem a difficult ministry, a witness to Jewish people will bring blessing to God, to the Jewish people themselves, and to the church.

Gerald Anderson observed, "As goes one's commitment to Jewish evangelism, so goes one's commitment to missions." In other words, if I am uncertain whether I should witness to Jewish people, I am probably uncertain about witnessing to *any*body. Anderson commented that it is all right to dialogue about one's faith with Jewish people, but he added that one must also *proclaim* (tell forth!) the good news of salvation through Messiah Jesus.

Bishop John Taylor commented that a Jewish woman wanted him to use his authority to persuade his denomination to give up its Jewish outreach ministry. He told her, "I have no authority to do that, for it was not mine, nor even the Church of England's, but Christ's gospel that we are entrusted with."

The motivation

God gives the motivation to witness to Jewish people about Messiah because:

1. It is in Messiah Jesus that salvation (total shalom) is found for all people who believe, both Jews and Gentiles.

2. Despite the tragic past record of Christians relating to Jews, it would be anti-Jewish not to share the gospel with Jews. We must witness humbly, yet confidently.

3. The whole family of God will be blessed as Jews become Messianic believers.

4. God has certainly not finished his work among and within the Jewish people, and we are to witness to Jews to help to accomplish God's purposes.

Samuel Isaac Schereschewski was a Jew born in Russian Lithuania in 1831. As a student he received a Hebrew copy of the New Testament produced by the London Missionary Society. He became a believer in Messiah, studied in seminary in the United States, joined the Episcopal church, and headed off to China. He was skilled with languages and translated the prayer book and the Old and New Testaments into Mandarin. For several years, until struck by a paralyzing illness, he was bishop of Shanghai. But despite his paralysis, Schereschewski continued Bible translation. When he could no longer use a pen, he could still type, using his two index fingers. Painstakingly he produced a revision of the Mandarin Old Testament and a translation of the complete Bible in the Wen-li dialect. He was considered one of the top orientalists in the world in the 19th century. What if no one had been available or willing to share a witness about Messiah Jesus with Samuel Schereschewski?[6]

---

6 Adapted from Louis Goldberg's *Our Jewish Friends* (1977), pp. 176-178.

Study questions for reflection and discussion

1. Review from this chapter the biblical motivation for a Christian witness to Jewish people and the objections to such a witness which some Christians have raised. How do you respond?

2. How can one affirm the exclusiveness of salvation only through Jesus and at the same time reach out with understanding and sensitivity to persons of various backgrounds?

3. How high a priority should a witness to Jewish people have within Christian missions and evangelism?

4. In *your own words*, what is the "good news of Messiah Jesus"? Consider how a person who is not familiar with Christian language might respond to your definition.

5. You might ask a Jewish friend or acquaintance to share with you about his or her faith. This may give you an opportunity to share your faith in return. Remember that prayer and dependency upon the Holy Spirit are important aspects of the Christian witness.

6. The religious faiths of Jewish people and Christian people are not unrelated. In anticipation of chapter two, ask yourself, "How is the Christian faith related to the Jewish faith?"

2

Christianity is Jewish!

Common roots?

"What do you believe?" an international Jewish reporter asked Edith Schaeffer. Edith responded by giving a two-hour overview of the Bible.

"And what do you call this religion?" the reporter questioned. "It sounds like a Jewish religion to me."

"Yes," Edith replied, "Christianity *is* Jewish."[1]

Perhaps you are surprised. You may consider Christianity to be basically a Gentile faith. You know there are some "Jewish Christians" around, but they seem few and far between.

Most *Jewish* people also think of Christians and Gentiles as one and the same. It is quite unheard of for a Jewish person to talk about a Jewish Christian. As far as many in the Jewish community are concerned, if a Jewish person professes faith in Jesus, he or she is no longer considered a Jew and is seen as a traitor.

Before Andrew Barron believed in Messiah, he rarely thought about Jesus. "I assumed he was Catholic," Andrew says. "I figured the Gentiles were looking for a way

---

1 From *Christianity Is Jewish* by Edith Schaeffer (Wheaton, IL: Tyndale, 1975), p.11. Edith Schaeffer's book paraphrases the story of the Bible from Genesis to Revelation, showing how God worked throughout both covenants to create a people for himself.

to be more like Jews, so they built a religion around a Jew who was Catholic."[2]

Christianity *is* Jewish! Jews and Christians have common roots. The spiritual ancestors of Gentile Christians are godly Jews.

The Jewish context of Christian faith

Every one of the writers of the Bible, with the likely exception of Luke, was Jewish. Even Luke had probably adopted Judaism as his faith.

Jesus was Jewish. He was not a blond, white European but an olive-skinned Middle Easterner. He lived his life in Judea and Galilee. His twelve disciples were Jewish.

Jesus celebrated Jewish festivals. He said he had come to fulfill the Jewish Law. The edge of his cloak touched by the woman needing healing was quite likely the fringes worn by an "observant" (see p. 65) Jewish man. (See Numbers 15:37-41 and Mark 5:27, 6:56.)

In the middle of a Jewish Passover seder (ceremonial meal), Jesus originated what Christians have come to call "communion." The bread he broke was unleavened matzo.

God anointed the early believers with the Holy Spirit during the Jewish Festival of *Shavuot* (Pentecost).[3] We often call that event "the birthday of the church."

The early church was primarily Jewish. Paul and his team, even as they reached out to Gentiles, were first of all concerned that Jews hear about Jesus.

We call Abraham the father of the Jewish people, although the name "Jew" actually comes from Judah, Abraham's great-grandson. The Hebrew Scriptures tell the story of the small nation of people through whom God chose to reveal himself to the world. God came as Savior to

---

2 From *Jesus for Jews*, edited by Ruth Rosen (San Francisco: A Messianic Jewish Perspective), 1987, p. 16.

3 Shavuot ("weeks") was the spring harvest festival. Pentecost, from the Greek, means 50th, referring to the counting to the 50th day during this Feast of Weeks. This festival also commemorates God's giving of the Law on Mt. Sinai.

the world through one particular Jewish person, Jesus of Nazareth, who was fully human and Jewish, and yet fully God—a mystery accepted by faith.

Jesus said to the woman of Samaria, "Salvation is from the Jews" (John 4:22). God chose to bring his salvation through the Jewish nation and the Jewish Savior, his Son. Christians owe a great debt to the Jews. There is no place for anti-Semitism.

The Bible come to life

Philip Bottomley, who formerly directed A Christian Ministry Among Jewish People (CMJ) in the U.S., uses artifacts and costumes to help the world and culture of the Bible come to life.[4] Once, dressed as a Jewish high priest, he explained to our church the meaning of the various parts of his attire. Philip showed how the symbolism is ful-

A model of a priest in traditional attire from the Hebrew tabernacle replica at Lancaster, Pa.

Jonathan Charles. Courtesy Herald Press

---

4 Rev. Bottomley's "Bible Come to Life" costume talks have been developed from CMJ/UK's "Bible Come to Life Exhibition" which began in 1891. The authentic Middle Eastern costumes he uses belong to this Exhibition.

filled in the Great High Priest Messiah Jesus and in our
lives as priests of God. How meaningful to note the high
priest's breastplate with the twelve gems representing the
twelve tribes of Israel. The high priest carried his people
"on his heart" before God in prayer.[5]

Another time, Philip dressed as John the Baptist and
burst into our service with the call to "Repent!" Using the
words of John, he presented a sermon "come to life" from
the ministry of John the Baptist. Philip described and modeled a camel hair coat like John would have worn. It was
not the furry animal skin worn by a wild man whom you
would have trouble taking seriously. It was a garment
worn by an ordinary village man. His message was rele-
vant to everyman.[6] Philip believes that John ate not the
locust insect, but the fruit pods of a locust tree. Again, this
would alter the common view of John as a wild man.
These are examples which demonstrate that understanding
the Jewish and Middle Eastern world of the Bible helps the
Bible come to life with new meaning for us. It is not a
Western book, although when understood its meaning is
applicable and adaptable to peoples of all cultures.

Near Lancaster, Pennsylvania, the Mennonite Church
has set up a full-scale replica of the Hebrew tabernacle in
the wilderness. A lecture-tour explains the laver of cleansing, the altar for burnt offerings, the furnishings (the table
of shewbread, the candlestick, and the altar of incense), the

---

5 The high priest's intricately woven white coat symbolized beauty, his
blue robe showed royalty, the bells and "pomegranates" on the bottom fringes of
the garment indicated prayers being heard and also fruitfulness. The apron's col-
ors hold significance: gold for righteousness and uniqueness—Jesus being the
unique Son of the Father, the righteous Messiah; blue for Godhead; scarlet for
humanity; and purple for the blending of the two. Thus Jesus, the God/Man, is
the perfect Mediator between God and man. The inscription on the turban head
band was "Holiness to the Lord." Messiah Jesus beautifully fulfilled these symbols. They represent the high calling of each believer as a priest of Messiah.

6 A related point is that John the Baptist's coat, if made on the narrow
looms of Judea, would have had a seam. Jesus, coming from Galilee where broad
looms were used, had a seamless robe, which the soldiers cast lots for at his crucifixion.

heavy curtain separating the holy place from the most holy place, the ark of the covenant, and the side and top coverings of the tabernacle. Some 33,000-34,000 people per year have been visiting the tabernacle in recent years. It is a powerful visual aid illustrating the Hebrew Scriptures. Christians are reminded of their roots in the Jewish faith and how Jesus beautifully and wonderfully filled full with meaning the symbols of the tabernacle, especially the presence of God among his people in Messiah Jesus. The curtain hiding the most holy place was torn from top to bottom when Jesus died. Now, through the atoning sacrifice of Jesus, believers can approach God directly with openness and confidence.

Model of the interior of the Tabernacle, showing the holy place with priest, the shewbread table, candlestick, and altar of incense.

Our faith is enriched

The tabernacle replica illustrates how understanding Jewish roots brings special meaning to the Christian faith. Consider now 1 Peter 2:9, 10:

> But you are a chosen people, a royal priesthood, a holy nation, a people belonging to God, that you may declare the praises of him who called you out of darkness into his wonderful light. Once you were not a people, but now you are the people of God; once you had not received mercy, but now you have received mercy.

These verses describe the New Covenant people of God in images of the First Covenant people of God. As at one time the Jewish nation did not exist as a people, so all people were scattered about in the world of spiritual darkness. God called together a people, beginning with Abraham. Just so, all believers in Jesus have been called together from various backgrounds to be a community of faith.

The Jewish people were chosen and remain special to God, for he called together this people to bring glory to him and to be a light to the nations.[7] God has chosen those within the New Covenant to also be a special people for him, to worship him and to be a witness to the world.

The Jewish nation was called to be kingly—to belong to God the King. They were called to be a priesthood, especially modeled in the priests, who represented the people to God. But the whole community was to be a priesthood to help bring the world to God. Even more so, those in the New Covenant community relate directly to God without human priests, through the work of Messiah Jesus. All are priests, to minister to each other and to help bring the world to God.

The people of Israel were to be holy, separated unto God from the pagan peoples around them. The New Cov-

---

7 Although a majority of the Jewish people are yet unbelieving, the glory of God will shine through this ancient people most gloriously in the great Jewish revival predicted in the Scriptures. See Romans 11.

enant community belongs to the Lord's kingdom, not a kingdom of this world.

These verses from 1 Peter illustrate how the Jewish imagery and background of a Scripture passage enriches understanding about the Christian faith. Christians are spiritual descendants of Abraham, the Father of the Jewish people, because Christian believers come to God by faith and act upon that faith with an obedient response to God, just as Abraham did. (See Romans 4:9-12.)

Hebrew wholism

The Jewish faith sees *both* body and spirit as important. In Hebrew thought, a person is an animated body, a body made alive by spirit. Classical Greek understanding saw a person as an embodied spirit, a spirit trapped in a body of flesh.

Christians influenced by Greek thought often think only "spiritual" things are important—making sure people's "souls" are saved and their "hearts" are made holy.

When Christians understand the Jewish *and* biblical view of the person and the world, they will not emphasize only the transformation of the spirit by the Spirit of God. They will work for justice for the oppressed and dispossessed, reconciliation for peoples in conflict, and caretaking of the environment. They will feed the hungry, house the homeless, strive to end war, conserve natural resources,[8] *all the while* pointing people to a relationship of shalom with God through Messiah Jesus.

Body and soul, matter and spirit—belong together! It is a Jewish insight which brings richness to the Christian faith community.

---

8 The New Age Movement has some similar emphases, but Christians find their source of direction and power in Messiah the Lord. See Luke 4:18-19.

Our witness is enhanced

Christian faith is not something radically different from Jewish faith, if one remembers that "radical" refers to "roots." There is continuity between the two. The First Covenant led into the New Covenant as God progressively revealed himself to his people, finally and supremely through Jesus. The continuity provides bridges which can lead into opportunities of witness for Messiah.

Yet there is also a difference between the Covenants because of Jesus. He *is* the *Connector* of the two covenants, but only as he is accepted as such. A Jewish shopkeeper said to me that the difference between the two of us is Jesus! How true!

Stories from the Hebrew tabernacle replica demonstrate how the Jewish roots of Christian faith can lead to witnessing opportunities. A Jewish man who came to see the tabernacle commented afterward, "As a Jew, I may not enter a Christian church, but this was beautiful. You really have something here. I want to return."

A Jewish woman who believed in Messiah bubbled with joy. "This is wonderful," she said. "I must bring my mother to see it. She doesn't know the Lord yet."

One Ascension Day, a Jewish couple visited with their two daughters. The girls had a school vacation day; it was the festival of Shavuot (Pentecost). The younger daughter asked, "What is the name and meaning of the *Christian* holiday?"

The mother chimed in, "It's called Ascension Day, and it commemorates the day when the Lord went up to heaven."

The child's next question was, "When did the Lord come down?"

"I did not say he came down; I only said it was the day when he went up," the mother replied.

The girl thought only a moment before she said, "But mother, we know that anything that goes up must first have been down. I only want to know . . . when did the Lord come down?"

"We must not detain the guide," the parents told their daughters. "We'll explain more in the car."

The guide was reminded that "a little child shall lead them" and prayed that as the parents searched for honest answers to their daughter's questions, they would be drawn to the truth of Jesus.

At the conclusion of one tabernacle lecture, a retired couple remained behind to privately ask their guide, "Do you believe the Old or the New Testament?"

"Both," the guide replied.

"That is what our son believes," the couple said. "We are Orthodox Jews, and we've felt a lot of anguish since our son has believed in Jesus as the Messiah. Some of our friends told us to have a funeral and disinherit him. But we couldn't do that; he's our son.

"We've just come from visiting him. There was so much love, joy, and peace evident in our son's home.

"Would you be able to give us a Bible with both Testaments in simple English? We don't read Hebrew very well."

When the guide gave them a *Good News Bible*, the couple was delighted and promised, "We'll read it, because we're sure it will help us understand our son and his new way of life."

The witness about Jesus is not an invitation to convert from Jewishness to Christianity, but to turn from sinfulness to salvation in Jesus. Jewish believers in Jesus are still Jewish—Messianic Jews! This is an "impossibility" in the eyes of many other Jews, but it should not be problematic for Christians. (Gentiles who believe in Jesus are still Gentiles!) Christians who understand their Jewish roots welcome Messianic believers into the community of God's people. Whether Jewish or Gentile, all believers in Messiah Jesus are "Messianic" believers!

Common roots

The roots and heritage of the Christian faith and community are Jewish. It is essential to know this background in order to:

1. understand the world and culture of the Bible;
2. appreciate the theology of Christian faith;
3. and relate and witness to Jewish friends and acquaintances (being alert to anti-Semitism).

Study questions for reflection and discussion

1. Identify illustrations, parables, or terminology in the Scriptures which are part of the Jewish context of the Bible that you have difficulty understanding. (Examples might be: Levites, marriage customs of the "ten virgins" parable, Pharisees, or Zion.) Use a Bible dictionary or Bible encyclopedia to do some research.

2. Consider concepts such as: covenant, priesthood, scapegoat, and Messiah. Consult a Bible dictionary to help you understand the Jewish background of these terms that are important to Christian faith.

3. If it is possible, plan a visit to the Hebrew Tabernacle replica at Lancaster, Pennsylvania. (The tabernacle is at the Mennonite Information Center, 2209 Millstream Road, Lancaster, PA 17602-1494. The phone number is: 717-299-0954.)

4. *In your own words*, how do you explain the relationship between the Old Testament (Hebrew Scriptures) and the New Testament?

5. Are the festivals of the Hebrew Scriptures, special events which God directed his people to celebrate, confusing and puzzling to you? Do they have meaning for Gentile Christian believers? Explore the rich significance of these festivals outlined in the next two chapters.

3

Come, let's celebrate!
Part I—The Fall Festivals and Hanukkah

God's people celebrate!

"I have trekked all across the United States, walking for peace, and to find a Feast of Tabernacles booth in a Christian church deeply touches me." That was the response of a Jewish peace walker when she entered Alpha Mennonite Church in central New Jersey and discovered a *sukkah* (Feast of Tabernacles booth) set up there. She was moved to see a Christian church appreciating her Jewish heritage.

The Feast of Tabernacles is also part of the Christian heritage, for the roots of Christianity are Jewish. The festivals of the Hebrew Scriptures provide a wealth of meaning for the Christian's experience with God. They are great opportunities for celebration.

People may celebrate Thanksgiving with turkey and stuffing and New Year's Day with parades and football games. They may thrill with excitement when their favorite team wins a World Series championship or a space shuttle lifts off successfully. Should not God's people joyfully celebrate their faith in him? Celebrations are an excellent way to pass on to our children a faith that exalts God's majesty, faithfulness, caring provision, and salvation.

In addition to Good Friday, Easter, Thanksgiving, and Christmas, the biblical festivals provide excellent opportunities for meaningful celebrations in praise to the goodness of God. In this chapter, we will look at the fall festivals, the "high holy days" of the Jewish calendar which occur in September and October. They begin with the Feast of Trumpets, lead into the Day of Atonement, and conclude with the Feast of Tabernacles. We will also consider Hanukkah. In the next chapter we will look at festivals of late winter and spring: Purim, Passover/Unleavened Bread, and Pentecost, plus the weekly Sabbath celebration.[1,2]

Messianic Pastor Richard Nichol blowing the shofar (ram's horn) which he called the "AT&T of the ancient world"

1 Whether or not Gentile believers should fully embrace the celebration of Jewish festivals is a question for discussion. Some believe these are national *Jewish* holidays. Others affirm them as celebrations for *all* God's people. But at least occasional participation can enrich the faith and biblical understanding of Gentile believers.

2 A chart in the back of this book shows the dates for several years for the Jewish holidays discussed in these two chapters.

A season of remembrance and repentance

The Feast of Trumpets is called that because of the blowing of the shofar (ram's horn) in celebrating this Jewish New Year festival. Its Hebrew name is *Rosh Hashanah*, which means "head of the year."

> The Lord said to Moses, "Say to the Israelites: 'On the first day of the seventh month you are to have a day of rest, a sacred assembly commemorated with trumpet blasts. Do no regular work, but present an offering made to the LORD by fire.'" (Leviticus 23:23-25)

The seventh month starts the economic year, the end of the old harvest year and the beginning of the new harvest year. However, this New Year's celebration has spiritual implications as well.

It celebrates God as Creator and King, asks him to remember his people, and petitions the people to remember their God. The haunting call of the ram's horn is a call to rest, remember, and repent. The bend of the ram's horn reminds one to bend in humility and repentance before a holy God.

In the Scriptures, the blowing of the trumpet is also associated with events yet to come—the judgment of God and the appearing of the Lord in his glory to complete the drama of salvation. (See Zephaniah 1:14-16 and Matthew 24:30, 31.)

Traditionally, the Jewish community observed the whole month preceding Rosh Hashanah plus the following ten days as a forty-day period of preparation for the Day of Atonement. This was a time to search one's life to prepare for God's forgiveness. The ceremony of *Tashlich* (Hebrew for "you shall cast into the seas") has been a traditional part of celebrating Rosh Hashanah. To symbolize casting away sin, crumbs of bread are thrown into a river where there are fish. The fish, with constantly open eyes, are symbolic of God's watchful eyes. Or, an alternate symbolism is that just as fish can be tricked and caught, so we humans can be deceived and entrapped by evil. Casting bread, or stones, into the sea reminds one that God casts away sin which has been repented of into the sea of his forgetfulness.

Who is a God like you, who pardons sin and forgives the transgression of the remnant of his inheritance? You do not stay angry forever but delight to show mercy. You will again have compassion on us; you will tread our sins underfoot and hurl all our iniquities into the depths of the sea. (Micah 7:18, 19)

This ceremony, which a family or a small group could reenact, is usually followed by a meal including honeycake, symbolizing the sweetness of God's forgiveness.

A beautiful example of God's provision that is associated with the Feast of Trumpets is the story of his providing a ram when Abraham was about to sacrifice Isaac on Mount Moriah. The offering of Isaac is traditionally thought to have occurred on Rosh Hashanah on the mountain where the temple would later be built and sacrifices for sin offered. Those who remember the story recall Abraham's faith, his willingness to obey, and Isaac's obedient submission. They ask God to honor them with the same mercy he showed to Abraham and Isaac. They celebrate God's provision of a ram. Isaac's salvation was like a resurrection! There is cause to celebrate by blowing on the ram's horn.

Isaac, son of Father Abraham, foreshadowed Messiah Jesus, Son of Father God, in laying down his life as a sacrifice. Isaac's death, however, was not required, as the ram became his substitute. Jesus actually gave his life as an offering for sin for all people who believe and repent. Isaac was in a sense resurrected from the dead; Jesus was *actually* resurrected!

A day of forgiveness

On the tenth day of the seventh month comes the Day of Atonement, Yom Kippur, the holiest day of the Jewish year. *Yom Kippur* means "day of covering" (covering of sin by blood sacrifice of animals). Yom Kippur is a day of mourning and fasting for sin. It is also a day to stand in awe of God's holiness and to carefully prepare to receive his forgiveness.

On this day, the high priest entered the holy of holies, where the ark of the covenant rested. The ark was a wooden chest, originally containing the stone tables of the Law, a bowl of manna, and Aaron's almond rod which had budded. In that tabernacle and temple era, before the Holy Spirit was poured out, the presence of God centered in the most holy place, especially upon the mercy seat, the top cover of the ark, over which hovered two sculptured cherubim.

A model of the ark of the covenant

On Yom Kippur, the high priest carefully bathed his whole body and dressed in special garments of linen.[3] In addition to the twice-daily burnt offerings and other festive sacrifices, there were the special Day of Atonement

---

3 For your own study, refer to Leviticus 16.

offerings of a young bull (for the sins of the high priest, his household, and the priesthood) and of two goats (for the sins of the people).

The high priest first entered the holy of holies with burning coals and incense. He poured the incense on the live coals so that the cloud of sweet burning incense, representing the high priest's prayers for forgiveness, would cover the mercy seat. The high priest would enter the holy of holies a second time with blood from the slain bull, carefully sprinkling it once, and then seven more times, on the mercy seat as atonement for his sin.

Lots were cast on the two goats to determine which one was to be sacrificed. The high priest then went into the most holy place a third time and sprinkled the blood of the sacrificed goat on the mercy seat, this time for the people's sin. Then the high priest would confess the sins of the people upon the head of the live goat, the scapegoat, and this goat would "carry away" the people's sins as it was led into the wilderness, there to be banished and forsaken.[4]

The Day of Atonement pointed toward the coming of God's Messiah, Jesus, who would be both the perfect high priest and the perfect sacrifice. Jesus represents his people to God as the one who sacrificed himself to atone for our sins (as the slain goat) and also carried our sins away (as the banished scapegoat). Because he was the perfect sacrifice, he offered himself once for all time and for all people who trust in him for salvation. Other blood sacrifices need no longer be offered.

At the time of Messiah's death, the great curtain concealing the holy of holies was torn from top to bottom. Those who turn from their sin can now approach God directly through Jesus to find forgiveness and comfort. (See Hebrews 4:14-16.) About forty years after Jesus' death, the

---

4 With no more temple and no more animal sacrifices, Jewish people have often substituted prayers, fasting, and giving of charity as means for atonement of sin. These, of course, cannot truly atone for sin.

temple itself was destroyed. While recognizing this as a tragedy of military conquest, the Messianic believer sees that God has no need for a "temple made with hands," because God "tabernacles" among his people in his Son. His Son's death (and resurrection!) brought fulfillment to the temple sacrifices.

God now dwells in his redeemed and forgiven people by the Holy Spirit. God's people are his temple! God is showing that a "holy people" surpasses the holiness of a special place. (See Acts 7:44-50 and 2 Corinthians 6:16.)

For Messianic believers, the Day of Atonement celebrates the perfect sacrifice of Messiah Jesus, and the forgiveness received through him. Believers could spend it as a day of fasting and prayer for Jewish people and all people who have not appropriated for themselves the sacrificial death of Messiah, God's offer of forgiveness for sin, and a new relationship with God and his people.

One could plan a Messianic Yom Kippur service during a twenty-four-hour period of fasting which would focus on confession of sin, thanksgiving for Messiah's once-for-all atonement for sin, and praying for the lost. A group or family meal could break the fast (literally, a "break-fast").

Following forgiveness comes a time of rejoicing. Thus we turn to the Feast of Tabernacles.

A season for rejoicing and thanksgiving

Following the somber time of the high holy days, the festival of *Sukkot* ("tabernacles" or "booths") is a time of festivity and joy. It begins five days after the Day of Atonement. In those five days, the "booth" or shelter can be built. In fact, the first steps of its construction are often taken at the close of Yom Kippur. This festival was a seven-day, family "camping" adventure. Together with Passover and Pentecost, the Feast of Tabernacles was one of the three festivals when Jewish men were to make a pilgrimage to Jerusalem. God had given these instructions:

"'On the first day you are to take choice fruit from the trees, and palm fronds, leafy branches and poplars, and rejoice before the LORD your God for seven days.... Live in booths for seven days: All native-born Israelites are to live in booths so your descendants will know that I had the Israelites live in booths when I brought them out of Egypt. I am the LORD your God.'" (Leviticus 23:40, 42, 43)

As the family lived in the temporary shelter constructed of a pole frame with leafy coverings, often gaily decorated with colorful fruits and vegetables, they celebrated several themes:

1. God's faithfulness to past and present generations;

2. God's provision of the harvest of food, which was being reaped;

3. and God's protection; he was, and is, the people's security.

The booth or hut itself was a visual reminder of the temporary shelter-dwellings of their Jewish ancestors during the wilderness trek. The decorations of fruits and vegetables hanging from the leafy boughs of the shelter were also visual aids, portraying the food of another year's harvest, a provision from God. Through the roof of this tem-

Celebrating under a sukkah (Feast of Tabernacles booth)

porary shelter, one could see the sky, dramatically symbolizing that material things (houses, wealth, or military armaments) were not the "security" of God's people. They were to trust in God himself!

God's people often did not celebrate the festivals he had set up for them. When there was revival of worship, celebration of the festivals was sometimes a part of the revival. For example, when the exiles who had returned from Babylon heard Ezra read from God's Word (Nehemiah 8), the people discovered God's instructions for the Feast of Tabernacles. They immediately built booths and celebrated for a week, as Ezra continued to read the Scriptures to them.

By the time Jesus came on the scene, a water ceremony had become associated with the festival of Sukkot. Water was drawn from the pool of Siloam and poured out around the altar at the temple, accompanied by prayers for rain for the next year's harvest. This drawing and pouring of water also symbolized the people's anticipation of the coming Holy Spirit. (See Isaiah 12:3 and Joel 2:28.) The priests circled the altar, pouring out the water, once each day for the first six days of the feast. On the seventh day, they circled the altar seven times. And on this day the people cried out *"Hosheanah!"* ("Save now!"). It was likely to this day that John referred when he wrote:

> On the last and greatest day of the Feast, Jesus stood and said in a loud voice, "If anyone is thirsty, let him come to me and drink. Whoever believes in me, as the Scripture has said, streams of living water will flow from within him." By this he meant the Spirit, whom those who believed in him were later to receive. Up to that time the Spirit had not been given, since Jesus had not yet been glorified. (John 7:37-39)[5]

---

5 There is an eighth day connected to the Sukkot festival. The eighth day is *Simhat Torah* (the rejoicing in the Law). Traditionally on this day the last chapter of Deuteronomy and the first chapter of Genesis are read, showing that the circle of Torah (five books of Moses) is eternal, without end or beginning.

Jesus was making an unabashed announcement of his Messiahship! The prophet Zechariah (in chapter 14) speaks of a time when the nations of the world will come to Jerusalem to celebrate Sukkot. The second coming of Messiah may be further fulfillment of this festival when Messiah, full of glory, comes to tabernacle among his people forever.

In the meanwhile Messianic believers can joyfully celebrate Sukkot and its grand themes of thanksgiving to God for his faithful provision and trust in God as the ultimate and supreme source of security. In a world where stock market "securities" crash and where the stockpiling of weapons for national "security" simply escalates the threat of war, people need the true security which God provides!

A few years ago we set up a simple *sukkah* (singular of sukkot) in the front of our church sanctuary. We discussed its meaning in our men's prayer fellowship. A Jewish friend who joined us that morning expressed his appreciation that we included this Jewish festival in the life of our congregation. I integrated this festival with the Thanksgiving season and encouraged members of the congregation to tack up notes of thanks to God on a bulletin board set up with the booth. Actually, the Feast of Tabernacles likely provided the background for the first Thanksgiving feast in the "New World," which the pilgrims thought of as a "new Promised Land."

You may wish to set up a sukkah in your backyard and celebrate the festival as a family. Some Jewish families in our Philadelphia community construct a shelter of canvas or plyboard walls, topped with leafy branches, in their yard. They may eat a number of meals in it during the week of Sukkot, as weather permits.[6]

---

6 In her book, *Celebrate the Feasts*, Martha Zimmerman gives detailed instructions for a family celebration of Sukkot. She includes menus and recipes. (See note at end of chapter.)

The Feast of Lights

The last festival we shall consider in this chapter is *Hanukkah* (which means "dedication"). Hanukkah is mentioned only once in Scripture, with reference to Jesus being present at the temple at the time of Hanukkah and talking with fellow Jews. (See John 10:22-24.)

The story of Hanukkah belongs to the Intertestamental period and is told in the books of the Maccabees in the Apocrypha. Antiochus Epiphanes (nicknamed the "madman" because of occasional fits of insanity) became king of Syria in 175 B.C.E. and ruled over the Jewish people. He performed horrible atrocities against the Jews. He had a pig sacrificed on the temple altar and its blood sprinkled in the holy of holies. Broth from the pig's cooked meat was poured on sacred scrolls of the Law. Antiochus announced, "I am God!" and dared the Jews to defy his pagan decrees.

A group of Jewish guerrillas began to fight back against Antiochus's men. Judah Maccabee was a particularly able leader of these guerrilla fighters. Eventually they defeated the Syrians and entered Jerusalem to find the holy city dirty and desecrated by statues of Greek gods and goddesses. They discovered that swine had been offered on the temple altar.

The people scrubbed and cleaned the temple and prepared it for rededication. Only a little holy oil could be found with which to light the great Menorah (candelabrum) of the temple. But miraculously the Menorah's lights kept burning for eight days.

The festival of Hanukkah, held in December, celebrates this dedication of the temple in 165 B.C.E. An eight-candle menorah is used, with an additional candle lit each successive night of the eight-day festival. It is again a family event with gift-giving, special foods, and playing a game with a top called a dreidel. The dreidel was used as a ploy to make unsuspecting Syrian soldiers in Antiochus's time think that Jewish students, gathered to study Torah by memory, were harmlessly playing an innocent game. There are now four Hebrew letters on the dreidel, one on each side of the four-sided top.[7] They are the first letters of four Hebrew words whose translation is, "a great miracle happened there."

Messianic believers can celebrate Messiah Jesus' coming as a fulfillment of Hanukkah. He said, "I AM the Light of the world." He is the greatest deliverer. He comes to cleanse and renew the lives of those who dedicate themselves to him. Hanukkah is a reminder that God is the great Provider who can use little things and insignificant people to bring about great miracles. He is Savior and Lord! The themes of Hanukkah can be integrated with the Messianic meaning of Christmas, enriching its celebration.

Celebration and fulfillment

We need to deliberately integrate celebration into our worship. It lifts our hearts from the routine to exalt the majesty of God. In the festivals of Rosh Hashanah, Yom Kippur, Sukkot, and Hanukkah there are themes and symbols which provide ways and means to practice such celebration. It is a rich heritage. Let Jewish and Gentile believers not neglect these Jewish roots while at the same time affirming Messiah Jesus, who fills these festivals full with meaning.

---

7 Players take turns spinning the dreidel. The letter on the side of the top facing up when it stops spinning determines whether the player takes all or half of the coins or whatever is in the "pot," whether one needs to give to the pot, or does nothing.

Study questions for reflection and discussion

1. Avail yourself of copies of books such as these for further study:

   a. *All About Jewish Holidays and Customs* by Morris Epstein (Ktav Publishing House, Inc., 1970)

   b. *The Fall Feasts of Israel* by Mitch and Zhava Glaser (Moody Press, 1987)

   c. *Celebrate the Feasts* by Martha Zimmerman (Bethany House Publishers, 1981). This is especially good for practical help for Messianic believers, Gentile and Jewish, who would like to celebrate the festivals at home or in the congregation.

2. Discuss ways in which these festivals could be celebrated in your home or congregation to help the Bible and your faith come alive with new meaning.

3. Consider whether there is a Jewish friend whom you could invite to share with you how one or more of these festivals are celebrated in his or her home and/or synagogue.

4. Look in the Bible, using a Bible encyclopedia, for references to these festivals. Note ways in which Jesus fulfills the themes of the festivals.

4

Come, let's celebrate!
Part II—Purim, the Spring Festivals, and the Sabbath

A Time for family

"My husband Nevin has found the Passover so meaningful, and it helps him understand the Bible," says Bonita, a Jewish believer in Messiah. Bonita and Nevin, a Gentile believer, regularly celebrate Passover with her Reformed Jewish family. The ties of family help overcome the barrier of her Messianic faith. Bonita does not want to lose the rich heritage of her Jewish roots. She and Nevin hope to pass it on to their young children.

Jewish festivals are family and community events. In a day when family and community are disintegrating, these kinds of celebrations provide for renewal in family and community life. A camp-out in a *sukkah*, an evening of family celebration around the Passover table, or a special weekly meal at the beginning of Sabbath when Dad praises Mother and touches his children in blessing, positively influence family life.

"Messianic Gentile" believers may enjoy incorporating some of the festivals, or aspects of them, into family and congregational life.[1] Three Jewish festivals fall in late winter and spring: Purim, Passover, and Pentecost.

Purim: a holiday of happiness

Purim falls in February or March. The Purim story comes from the book of Esther (Hadassah in Hebrew). "Purim" means "lots." It refers to Haman casting a lot to choose the date when he would carry out his scheme to destroy the Jewish people.

King Ahasuerus, angered by his queen's refusal to pleasure his drunken state and exhibit herself before the banqueting dignitaries who were his guests, issued a decree to find a new queen. Esther, sent by her cousin Mordecai who had adopted her, was one of the many young women who came to the palace at Shushan. The king chose this beautiful Jewish woman to be his new queen.

In the king's court was the proud Haman who had been promoted to a position of prominence over the princes. He became furious at Mordecai, a servant at the king's gate who refused to bow down before Haman. In his rage, Haman decided he wanted all of Mordecai's people, the Jews, destroyed. He told the king there was a group of people whose laws were different from the king's laws, and he persuaded the king to order that these people be killed.

Mordecai told Queen Esther what was to occur. He urged her to go to the king to plead on behalf of her people. The king listened, became enraged that Haman would plot to kill the queen's people, and ordered Haman hanged. The king issued another decree allowing the Jews to avenge themselves against those determined to destroy them. Instead of the 13th day of the month of Adar being a day of atrocity for the Jews, it became a day of victory over their enemies. The following day they celebrated.

---

1 See footnote 1 near the beginning of chapter 3. Note that there are additional Jewish festivals besides the eight major ones considered in these two chapters.

The 14th and 15th days of Adar on the Jewish calendar became the annual holiday of Purim. It is a time of merrymaking and pageantry. A special parchment scroll of Esther called the *Megillah* (meaning "rolled up"), is read in the synagogue, and every time Haman's name is uttered, the listeners make noise to drown it out. The holiday includes gift-giving and special foods, such as a three-cornered, poppy seed or plum jam pastry called "Haman's hat."

Purim is a time to celebrate God's preservation of his chosen people, although God's name never appears in the book of Esther. A number of special Purims celebrate other times when Jews were spared from forces of evil.

Passover: a time to rehearse God's salvation

Passover also celebrates God's deliverance. It anticipates the coming of Messiah. *Pesach* (the Hebrew term) recalls the death angel's "passing over" the Jewish homes in Egypt which had the blood of a lamb smeared on the doorframe. This last plague persuaded Pharaoh to let Moses and his people leave Egypt. God told Israel to prepare for this exodus by killing a lamb and putting some of its blood on the top and sides of the doorframe of the place where they would eat the roasted lamb with bitter herbs and unleavened bread. They were to dress for travel, with cloaks tucked into their belts, sandals on their feet, and a staff in hand. Israel left Egypt in a hurry, not using any manmade weapons to fight the Egyptian armies. God took them safely through the sea on dry ground. The pursuing Egyptians drowned behind them in the returning waters. Israel marched on into the wilderness, away from the slavery of Egypt, toward the land of promise.

The Jewish nation was commanded to celebrate the festivals of Passover and Unleavened Bread in the first month of the Jewish calendar (the month of *Nisan*, March or April on the Roman calendar). The Passover is a symbolic, ceremonial meal (called a seder) telling the story of

the exodus deliverance. The roasted lamb of earlier
Passovers recalls the lamb sacrificed and eaten at the exodus Passover. The bitter herbs represent the bitter suffering
of the Israelite slaves in Egypt. The unleavened bread
speaks of the haste with which they left Egypt, without
time to put yeast in the bread dough. During the seven-
day Unleavened Bread festival which immediately preced-
ed Passover, all yeast was to be removed from the home.
This also points to getting rid of sin in one's life, for in the
Scriptures yeast often symbolizes sin.

> "When you enter the land that the LORD will give you
> as he promised, observe this ceremony. And when
> your children ask you, 'What does this ceremony
> mean to you?' then tell them, 'It is the Passover sacri-
> fice to the LORD, who passed over the houses of the
> Israelites in Egypt and spared our homes when he
> struck down the Egyptians.'" (Exodus 12:25-27; see
> also Leviticus 23:4-8.)

In a practicing Jewish home today, the wife busies
herself with housecleaning prior to Passover. She removes
from the house any food with yeast, or locks it away in a
cupboard and sells it to a Gentile neighbor, to buy it back
later. The day before Passover the father of the home
searches the house with a candle, feather, spoon, and old
napkin, looking for crumbs of leaven. Mother has usually
left a few crumbs somewhere that he sweeps into the
spoon with the feather and wraps in the napkin to be burnt
in a community bonfire next morning.

At sundown that evening Passover begins. The dining
room table is set for the special ceremonial meal, with the
seder plate prominently displayed. This plate contains
symbolic foods. There is a roasted shank bone representing
the lamb (which can no longer be sacrificed since the
destruction of the temple). A hard-boiled egg substitutes
for the holiday sacrifice or peace offering of temple times.
It also symbolizes hope of new life. Bitter herbs are on the
seder plate: horseradish and lettuce, parsley, or celery.
These latter three may not seem bitter, but dipped in salt

water representing tears, they are a reminder of the bitterness of bondage. *Charoseth*, a sweet, reddish-brown mixture of chopped apples, nuts, raisins, cinnamon, and wine
or grape juice recalls the mortar the Israelite slaves used
for building.

Matzo, the unleavened bread, is also important to the
meal. Matzo are flat wafers whick look something like
saltine crackers. Wine[2] is sipped at four different intervals
throughout the meal. The *Haggadah* is the printed order of
service. The father's Haggadah is often a beautifully decorated book.

Candles are lit, and the participants lift the cup of
wine of sanctification to their lips. The host ceremonially
cleanses his finger tips. Each one receives a bit of lettuce,
parsley, or celery. A blessing is then recited, "Blessed art
thou, Lord God, King of the Universe, who createst the
fruit of the earth." The herb is dipped in salt water and
eaten. The host takes the middle matzo wafer from the
three wrapped in the folds of a napkin, breaks it, puts one
part back, and hides the other part in a napkin which he
places at another spot, perhaps in a pillow at his chair. The
pillow symbolizes eating the Passover in ease, not in slavery.

A child or several children ask questions about why
this night is different from other nights. Throughout the
meal participants read the story of God's deliverance of
Israel from Egypt and his faithfulness. They recite a poem
or song which recounts a number of God's saving acts, any
one of which "would have been sufficient," as the song
"Dayenu" says. The participants sip wine again, this second time to give thanksgiving and praise to God. They
recite two *Hallel* ("Praise") Psalms, the 113th and 114th.

---

2 If preferred, one may substitute grape juice when reenacting the
Passover.

All ceremonially cleanse their hands and then make a sandwich out of matzo, horseradish, and charoseth. Hardboiled eggs, often dipped in saltwater, frequently introduce the Passover dinner.

The dinner menu may include gefilte fish, matzo ball soup, stuffed and roasted fowl or beef, salads, vegetables, and a variety of desserts (but without yeast). The *aphikommen* ("that which comes last") is a further dessert. It is the hidden piece of matzo. In temple times, the lamb was to be the last thing eaten and remembered. Now, with no lambs, the taste of matzo is to linger last, as a substitute reminder of the lamb sacrifice. The children play a little game in searching for the hidden aphikommen. The child who finds it receives a small reward.

After the aphikommen is eaten, there is a lengthy prayer of thanksgiving, and the participants sip wine for the third time (the cup of redemption). There is a special cup for Elijah at the table, as well as an empty chair. A child opens the door, to see whether Elijah might be coming. (His coming is to precede Messiah's appearing.) With no sign of Elijah, the family recites the 115th to 118th Hallel Psalms, sings a hymn of benediction, and drinks from the cup of wine a final time (the cup of acceptance—God's acceptance of his people). One last prayer, for the rebuilding of Jerusalem, closes the seder.

It was in the midst of a Passover seder with his disciples that Jesus established what the church has come to call the Communion. At the beginning of the meal, although he was the host set apart by the initial ceremonial cleansing, he chose to model humble servanthood by taking the place of a slave and washing his disciples' tired, dusty feet. Even Judas would have been included. The "sop" handed to Judas (and to all the twelve) was likely the matzo dipped in bitter herbs and charoseth.

It is possible that Jesus may have been the first host ever to serve the aphikommen, when after supper he broke matzo, distributed it, and said, "This is my body broken for you." The cup he passed, when he said, "This cup is the new covenant in my blood, which is poured out for you," was probably the cup of redemption. At the close, they sang a hymn.

In his death and resurrection Jesus fulfilled the Passover. He was the sacrificed lamb, and he experienced the bitterness of suffering, represented by the bitter herbs. His body was broken as the matzo[3] was broken, and buried and resurrected as the aphikommen was "buried" (hidden) and then "resurrected" (recovered). Messiah poured out his blood to redeem his people, symbolized in the cup of redemption. Elijah (John the Baptist) had already appeared, preparing the way for Messiah.

The Israelites celebrated Passover *before* the exodus from Egypt, and Jesus celebrated the seder/communion *before* his death and resurrection. How amazing that God arranged for these celebrations to take place *before* these two great acts of his salvation! God calls his people to celebrate, not only after the fact, but in *anticipation* of the act of his saving grace.

If you have never participated in a Passover, seek out a Messianic Jewish friend or a knowledgeable Gentile Christian who could assist your family or congregation to observe or demonstrate this festive meal. Or do research yourself and plan your own celebration.

Shavuot: a time of anticipation

In the Middle Eastern world, the Passover and Unleavened Bread festivals coincided with the beginning of the grain harvest. On the first day of the week following

---

3 Manufactured matzo has holes pierced in it before baking and has a striped effect after baking. This can interestingly illustrate the piercing of Jesus' body by the nails and sword and the stripes received from the scourging. It is the middle piece of matzo which is broken and hidden. Just so, Messiah is the middle person of the Trinity.

Passover, the people were to present an omer (half-gallon) of barley at the temple as a firstfruits thanksgiving offering for the new season's harvest which was to come. (Barley was the first of the grains to ripen.) Very significantly, on that first day of the week following the Passover when Jesus died, he arose from the dead, the *firstfruits* of all those believers in Messiah who will also be resurrected.

> But Christ has indeed been raised from the dead, the firstfruits of those who have fallen asleep. (1 Cor. 15:20)

With this firstfruits offering, the people began counting off fifty days, at which time they offered firstfruits of the wheat harvest and of other produce. These offerings celebrated the holiday of *Shavuot*, or Pentecost.[4] According to tradition, Moses received the Law on Mt. Sinai fifty days after the exodus.

Devout Jews would stay up for a night preceding Shavuot, reading an anthology of Scriptures and sacred writings to recall the receiving of the Law. Worshipers read the book of Ruth. The Gentile Ruth modeled one who had personally received the Law of God for her own life, and the story is set in the midst of harvest-time. Milk and honey, symbolizing God's Word, are eaten in festive foods at Shavuot.

It was on the Festival of Shavuot that God poured out the Holy Spirit on the 120 believers gathered in Jerusalem. The pleasant weather at Pentecost time enabled a great number of travelers to make this trip. This anointing of the Spirit was the firstfruits promise of great things still to come for God's people.

One could plan interesting family or congregational activities to accompany a Shavuot celebration: for example, counting off fifty days with daily Scripture readings, leading up to Shavuot; presenting a special offering to the Lord

---

4 *Shavuot* is the Hebrew for "weeks," and this festival is also called the Feast of Weeks. Pentecost, meaning "50th," is the Greek name for the festival.

Candlelighting at the beginning of the Sabbath eve meal during a Shavuot banquet

of firstfruits from people's lives, endeavors, or income; or hold an all-night watch preceding Shavuot/Pentecost (with a variety of worship and "stay-awake" activities). See Martha Zimmerman's book, *Celebrate the Feasts*, for specific suggestions.

Sabbath: a weekly festival of rest and remembering

One winter Friday evening I was a guest of the Rich and Sue Nichol family of Needham, Massachusetts, as they celebrated their *Shabbat* (Sabbath) eve meal. It was a special occasion of welcoming the Sabbath, enjoying each other's presence, and blessing the family. The Nichol children helped explain the significance of the parts of this festive meal.

One can understand that a Messianic Jewish family such as the Nichols choose to celebrate this important tra-

dition of their Jewish heritage. Are there any particular
lessons from this celebration which other members of the
Christian community can benefit from?

Only on a few occasions has our family attempted
such a celebration on a Saturday evening in anticipation of
Sunday. Yet there are some important lessons that we as
believers can learn from the Jewish Sabbath.

We speak about TGIF (Thank God it's Friday!). The
work week is finally over, and the paycheck arrives. We
call Saturday and Sunday the "weekend," and usually fill
them up with all kinds of activities. Sometimes these full
weekends recreate us; sometimes they do not.

Traditionally the Jewish community has viewed the
Sabbath not as the weekend, but as the "middle," the central focus of the week. For three days one anticipates the
coming Sabbath, on the day itself one rests and celebrates,
and on the three days following one remembers the blessing of the Sabbath just past.

Do you recall the double celebration which God has
proclaimed in the Scriptures in establishing the Sabbath for
his people? First, the people were to remember God's rest
from his creating of the world:

> Remember the Sabbath day by keeping it holy. Six
> days you shall labor and do all your work, but the
> seventh day is a Sabbath to the LORD your God. On it
> you shall not do any work, neither you, nor your son
> or daughter, nor your manservant or maidservant,
> nor your animals, nor the alien within your gates. For
> in six days the LORD made the heavens and the earth,
> the sea, and all that is in them, but he rested on the
> seventh day. Therefore the Lord blessed the Sabbath
> day and made it holy. (Exodus 20:8-11)

Second, Israel was to remember the exodus:

> Remember that you were slaves in Egypt and that the
> LORD your God brought you out of there with a
> mighty hand and an outstretched arm. Therefore the
> LORD your God has commanded you to observe the
> Sabbath day. (Deuteronomy 5:15)

The Sabbath day was a time to rest from regular work, to worship God, to enjoy his creation, and to reflect on his salvation from the slavery of Egypt. Even the servants and animals and strangers were to rest. It was a day of justice and equality.

One welcomed and embraced the Sabbath, a gift from God, as a bride anticipates uniting with her bridegroom on their wedding day. Celebrating the Sabbath was a weekly renewing of one's covenant relationship with God.

The practicing Jewish family makes the Friday evening meal at the beginning of the Sabbath a special family event. The Jewish day begins at sunset and ends at sunset the following evening. Rest comes before work, rather than work before rest.

On Friday evening the table is set for company, and the "company" is one's own family. Mother has cleaned the house and prepared a special meal, perhaps with her family's help. As the family gathers around the table, she rises and lights two candles.

She shields her eyes with her hands as she prays, "Blessed are you, O Lord our God, King of the universe, Who has made us holy by your commandments, and commanded us to kindle the Sabbath lights."

Mother's role in this signifies a reversal of the role of the first mother, Eve, who turned her back on God's law and light and gave in to the tempter. The two candles represent creation and redemption. Extra candles add to the festivity of the occasion.

Father rises to bless his children, placing his hands on them one at a time. The traditional blessing for the boy is "May God make you like Manasseh," and for a girl, "May God make you like Sarah, Rebekah, Rachel, and Leah." Father could also create a down-to-earth, up-to-date blessing such as "David, may you do well in the big soccer game next week." Father also compliments his wife, using words from Proverbs 31, such as:

A wife of noble character who can find? She is worth
far more than rubies. Her husband has full confidence
in her and lacks nothing of value. . . . Her children
arise and call her blessed; her husband also, and he
praises her: "Many women do noble things, but you
surpass them all." Charm is deceptive, and beauty is
fleeting; but a woman who fears the LORD is to be
praised. (Proverbs 31:10-11, 28-30)

How meaningful to the children to hear such affirmation from their father each week and also to hear him com-
pliment their mother. And what a blessing for the wife to
hear her husband's words of praise.

The family then sings a song of peace or blessing. In
her adapted version of the Sabbath eve celebration, Martha
Zimmerman includes the words of "Bless Our Home"
(could be sung to a tune such as "Edelweiss"):

> Bless our home, bless our food;
> Come, O Lord, and sit with us;
> May our talk glow with peace,
> May your love surround us;
> Friendship and love, may they bloom and grow,
> Bloom and grow forever;
> Bless our home, bless our food;
> Come, O Lord, and sit with us.[5]

Father recites the Kiddush (a sanctification prayer)
over a cup of wine (you could use grape juice): "You are
blessed, Lord our God, King of the universe, you who cre-
ated the fruit of the vine."

A hand-washing ceremony follows, symbolizing dedication, and Father recites a blessing for the bread: "Blessed
are you, O Lord our God, King of the universe, who brings
forth bread from the earth."

The bread is not just any bread. Two loaves of *challah*
grace the table. These two twisted loaves represent the
double portion of manna gathered for the Sabbaths in the

---

5 From *Celebrate the Feasts* by Martha Zimmerman (Minneapolis: Bethany
House Publishers, 1981), page 38.

wilderness. The twisted shape of the loaves may also symbolize folded arms at rest. The bread on the table has been covered, remembering that in the wilderness the dew covered the manna each morning. Bread also reminds one that God is the provider of bread.

The bread is broken, not cut. At this point any knives on the table may be covered as an expression of the longing of the Jewish people for an end to swords and bloodshed. Believers may also recall the symbolism of Jesus' broken body.

The family then enjoys the meal, concluding with a prayer of grace and thanksgiving.

Synagogue services are held on Friday night and Saturday. At sunset on Saturday there is a ceremony of *Havdalah* (meaning "separation") when the Sabbath is ending and a new week is beginning. A cup of wine filled to overflowing represents the week's being filled to completion. After a prayer, two lighted candles twisted together are extinguished in the spilled wine. A spice box is passed around to symbolize that the fragrance of the Sabbath will carry people through the stresses of the following week.

For Jewish believers, the traditional Sabbath celebration can be integrated with new Messianic meaning. Messiah Jesus is the light of the world and the bread of life broken for us. He spilled his blood for us, and he calls us to live in peace.

Gentile believers could celebrate an adaptation of the special family meal and hold it on Saturday evening in preparation for Sunday worship, praying for the next day's service, and integrating the meaning Jesus brings to the symbols of the Jewish traditions. Even an occasional celebration could help us focus on bringing rest and joy into our weekly "Sabbath." The Hebrew word *Shabbat* means "rest." When Jewish people greet each other with "Good Sabbath!" they are wishing each other a time of good rest.

In our modern production-and-success-oriented society, can we relearn the meaning and practice of Shabbat-rest? With many stores and even some industries operating seven days a week, we hardly know the existence of a day of rest. Is it possible to revolutionize and transform the cycle of our weeks? Can we slow down and be recreated each weekend?

Sabbath is a time to step aside from our busy routine and celebrate God and his good gifts to us. If the weekend cannot be a Sabbath-rest for you, can you find another day for your personal Sabbath? Sabbath is a time for worship of God, enjoyment of family, fellowship with others, and personal recreation. Let us slow down our "rush" and make time for "rest."

Study questions for reflection and discussion

1. What creative ways can you use to remind yourself, your family, and your congregation of the saving acts of God? Especially, how can children be included? For the past several years, our congregation has performed a live, outdoor nativity pageant. It brings to life for us and our visitors the story of Messiah's birth. *Why Not Celebrate!* by Sara Wenger Shenk (Good Books, 1987) is full of creative ideas.

2. Make plans to celebrate a Passover in your home or congregation. *Christ In The Passover* (Moody Press, 1978) by Ceil and Moishe Rosen is a good resource. Martha Zimmerman's *Celebrate the Feasts* is also a good resource for this entire chapter.

3. What creative steps can you take to make the Sabbath or Sunday both a day of rest and also a day of remembering and renewal? Karen Burton Mains's *Making Sunday Special* (Word Books, 1987) is a very helpful book. She places Sunday in the context of Jewish Sabbath tradition and gives very practical suggestions.

4. How can traditions be kept alive with meaning rather than become dull and routine? (Jewish life and culture is full of traditions. We will take a further look in the next chapter.)

5

Being Jewish

A story of "Torah observance"[1]

Joel Stein is a young professional—a veterinarian.
Although his parents had become quite assimilated to
Midwest-American life, Joel had gradually reached back to
embrace his Jewish roots. Perhaps it was his long chats
with his aging and observant Jewish grandparents. Perhaps being two generations removed from new-immigrant
status, Joel felt more comfortable with being Jewish than
what his parents felt.

Three years ago, Joel and his young bride moved
from their small Midwest town, which had only a sprinkling of Jewish families, to a large city in the Northeast
United States. Here they settled into a neighborhood with
many Jewish families, a lot of them young families newly
interested in being "Torah-observant."

Joel and Miriam walk to synagogue on the Sabbath,
leaving their car parked at the curb for the day. They prepare food ahead of time, so they need not cook on Shabbat.
They place their lights on a timer and connect their phone
to an answering machine, to stay within Sabbath guide-

---

1 "Torah-observant" refers to keeping the traditional Jewish practices
based on the Torah (the Hebrew Scriptures) and is the preferred designation
for the commonly used term "orthodox."

lines. The Steins are delighted that their Jewish community is establishing an *eruv* (a large part of their neighborhood designated as "private domain"), marked by sturdy string attached to utility poles around the perimeter of this "community." This means the Steins can carry baby Hannah on the Sabbath to the synagogue or to visit friends several blocks away. Otherwise, they could not go out in "public" on the Sabbath as a family; Miriam would need to stay at home with the baby. But with the "eruv," the "public" neighborhood becomes a "private domain." They keep a kosher kitchen, reserving separate pans and dishes for dairy products and for meats, never serving these foods together. There are Kosher restaurants, even a Kosher pizza shop, nearby.

Although Miriam is an attorney, working part-time, she is content to live out the modest niche of a wife and mother in a Torah-observant community. She looks forward to the time when her children will attend the local Hebrew elementary school. She has visited the school and watched the boys and girls, in separate groups, praying aloud. As the children chanted, they bobbed rhythmically up and down (alternately approaching God in love and then withdrawing from him in awe).

Joel anticipates the time when two-year-old Daniel will be trained to think in the method of legal discussion, now thousands of years old, used to dialogue and debate intricate laws in the Talmud.[2] Perhaps, he muses, Daniel will collect and trade rabbi cards (portraying famous rabbis) with his neighborhood friends as avidly as he (Joel) did with baseball cards.

Joel and Miriam wonder whether their children will continue Torah-observance as they grow older. Might Hannah want to marry outside their community, bringing on a conflict reminiscent of Papa Tevye in *Fiddler on the Roof*?

---

2 The Talmud includes the Torah and commentaries on the Torah.

(Struggling to hold onto Jewish tradition, Tevye exclaims at one point, "If I bend anymore, I'll break!") Will Daniel want to go off to a secular university to study psychology or something equally mind-stretching, like the brilliant son in the rabbi's family in Chaim Potok's novel, *The Chosen?* At least in the meanwhile, Joel and Miriam reason, they are finding new meaning and joy as they rediscover for themselves their Jewish heritage.

Who is a Jew?

Moise Rosen, founder and leader of Jews for Jesus, says that if you ask four Jews that question, you will likely receive five different answers. One answer is that a Jew is a person born of Jewish parents (descendants of Abraham, Isaac, and Jacob), especially a person born to a Jewish mother. Having a Jewish mother may be emphasized because of the Scripture in Ezra which directed Jewish men to put away their non-Jewish wives. Another reason is that because of the frequent abuse of Jewish women by Gentile persecutors, many Jewish children were born of Gentile fathers. Emphasizing the Jewish line passing through the mother allowed these children of mixed parentage to find a place in the Jewish community.

An additional answer to the question, "Who is a Jew?" is that one who converts to Judaism is a Jew. That is somewhat controversial in the Jewish community. Orthodox Jews in Israel are unhappy with a High Court ruling which does not exclude Israeli citizenship for those who were converted to Judaism through a non-Orthodox rabbi.

Yet another answer is that a person who considers him/herself a Jew is Jewish. That definition is problematic to Jews when a Messianic Jew claims to be Jewish. In general, if one is an atheist or a Buddhist or a Hindu but still considers him/herself Jewish, that is acceptable. However, in most cases, a Jewish believer in Messiah Jesus is not considered a Jew by the Jewish community.

In terms of population, there are around fourteen and one-half million or more Jews in the world. The largest concentration, six million, live in the United States. About four and a half million live in Israel and about one million live in the former Soviet Union.

Cultural groups

There are two basic cultural groups of Jews around the world: the *Sephardim* and the *Ashkenazim*. Sephardic Jews are the earlier of the two groups; they were dominant in the Middle Ages, especially in the Spanish Golden Age of Judaism (11th and 12th centuries). Their roots were in the Mediterranean world and Spain and before that in Babylonia and Persia. They were scholarly and leisurely, interested in science and in poetry. One famous Sephardic scholar, who did most of his work in Egypt, was Maimonides (d. 1204). He wrote about traditional Jewish beliefs, outlining thirteen principles of faith, and his work is still important today.

The Ashkenazim Jewish cultural group is rooted in central and eastern Europe. They embraced the Yiddish language, a mixture of German and Hebrew, using Hebrew letters. The majority of Jewish people in the world today are related to this cultural group. One Ashkenazim leader of the early 1700s, Baal Shem Tov ("Master of the Good Name"), felt that Orthodox Judaism did not need to be dull and legalistic. He emphasized emotions, joyful expression, and mysticism, leading to the *Hasidic* movement, which continues to this day.

There are other, small Jewish cultural groups, such as the Samaritans (a mixed Jewish-Gentile group) and the *Felashas* (black Jews) of Ethiopia.

Religious groups

The *Orthodox* Jews are the most traditional in doctrine and practice. God is one, he has especially chosen the Jews as his people, and he will extend his rule over the world.

In real life, what one practices is more important than what one believes. In other words, if you practice Orthodox Jewish traditions, you are considered to be Orthodox Jewish. The study of Torah (the 39 books of the Hebrew Scriptures) and the Talmud (commentary on the Torah by scholarly rabbis of the past) is very important to the Orthodox. The "Torah-observant" Jewish person wants to keep the Law of Moses and to use traditional forms of liturgy in worship.

The Hasidic Jews are the ultra Orthodox. "Hasid" means "pious." They may appear very pious, with distinctive black clothing, long coats, wide and furry hats, beards, and side curls worn by some Hasidim. However, their Orthodox theology and pious appearance springs to expressive life, full of joy and emotion. Dancing is a normal expression. Their worship is vibrant. The Hasidim are to Judaism what the "charismatics" are to Christianity. An Hasidic rabbi (often called "Rebbe") is highly revered, almost worshipped, and even looked to as a worker of miracles.

The *Lubavitchers* are one of the Orthodox sects. They are zealous Jewish missionaries and revivalists. Vehemently anti-Christian, they promote a "Jews for Judaïsm" movement to counteract the work of Jewish evangelism outreaches such as "Jews for Jesus." The goal of the Lubavitcher Jews is to make Judaism attractive and to stir up among Jewish young people a passion for practicing the faith of their parents and grandparents.

The *Conservative* Jews are the religious center of Judaism, between the very traditional Orthodox Jews and the liberal Reform Jews. They are not reacting to the traditionalism of the Orthodox so much as they are to the liberalism of the Reform branch. It was felt that Reform Judaism had become too progressive, and the Conservative Jewish school was a move back towards Jewish Orthodoxy. It is more flexible than the Orthodox, however. Jewish immigrants to America around the turn of the century became the ground swell of the Conservative movement, which had begun in the mid-19th century in Europe and America.[3] These were Jews who wanted to adapt to American life but at the same time keep many of the traditional Jewish practices. They forged a road between Orthodox Judaism, deeply devoted to the law of the Torah, and Reform Judaism, quite critical of Scripture and tradition.

A significant segment (perhaps 40 percent of those affiliated with a synagogue) of American Jews today are Conservative. Sabbath practices are not so strict as the Orthodox. It is permissible to drive a car and use electricity on the Sabbath. The synagogue sermon can be in the vernacular language instead of Hebrew. Men and women sit together in the synagogue. The philosophy of Conservative Judaism says one can change in keeping with the times, while still maintaining a commitment to Torah and traditional Jewish practices.

Reconstructionism is a small sub-group of Conservative Judaism. God is seen as a cosmic force rather than a personal being with whom one can relate. Reconstructionists include elements of traditional Judaism.

. The *Reform* branch of Judaism emerged in the 19th century, especially in Germany, founded by Moses Mendelssohn. Reform Judaism wanted to bring Jewish faith and practice into the modern world. It criticizes traditional interpretations of Scripture and often views God as an impersonal entity. Many traditional Jewish practices have been discarded. Reform Judaism emphasizes the ethics over the doctrines of Jewish faith. There is concern for justice in human society.

Reform worship liturgy can be in the language of the people, rather than in Hebrew. Women can become rabbis. Early in the Reform movement, a return to Zion was downplayed, but that has changed with the rise of the state

---

3 At first called "Historical Judaism," the movement came to be called "Conservative Judaism" by the early 20th century in America.

of Israel. Reform Judaism is the liberal branch of Judaism, although there are varieties of thought and practice. Reform Judaism had made large inroads among American Jews, but with the emergence of Conservative Judaism, that has changed.

Messianic Jews are another grouping. A later chapter will look at this growing movement of Jews who profess faith in Jesus as Messiah.

Secular Jews complete the spectrum. They may be cultural Jews who celebrate Passover, for example, as a cultural or family holiday, just as non-Christian Gentiles celebrate Christmas without religious meaning. They are basically unaffiliated with any of the Jewish religious groups. In the aftermath of the Holocaust, many would deny that there is a God, at least a God who cares or is able to make a difference in the world. The life of secular Jews revolves around a Jewish community center rather than a synagogue. The majority of Jews in Israel are secular, which makes for a continuous conflict between them and the Orthodox segment of the Israeli populace (e.g. on matters related to Sabbath observance).

Religious practices

The center of Jewish Orthodoxy is the study of *Talmud*. The Talmud consists of the Torah as well as the Mishnah and the Gemara, commentaries on the Torah.

The *Torah* is technically the five books of Moses, Genesis through Deuteronomy (the Pentateuch). However, "Torah" has come to refer to the whole of the Hebrew Scriptures and even to traditions attached to it. Another term for the Hebrew Scriptures is the *Tenach*, an acronym for Torah, Neviim, and Ketuvim.[4]

---

4 The Neviim are the Prophets (both former prophets: Joshua, Judges, Samuel, and Kings, and the later prophets: the "major" and "minor" prophets, except Daniel). The Ketuvim are the Writings: Job, Psalms, Proverbs, and everything else not included in the Torah (Pentateuch) or the Neviim.

The *Mishnah* is a commentary on the Torah. For many years this commentary was passed on orally. If you lived in Ezra's day and desired to be a religious leader, you needed to commit the Mishnah to memory. The Mishnah developed throughout the pre-New Covenant era and into Jesus' day, as the contributions of various sages were added to it. Some of the sayings are similar to teachings of Jesus in the Sermon on the Mount. Finally, by 200 C.E., the Mishnah was codified in writing, to preserve it for the Jewish community that was being dispersed throughout the world.

The *Gemara* is a commentary on the commentary, the Mishnah. There is a shorter Palestinian version, compiled "on the run" during a time of persecution, and a longer and more authoritative Babylonian version, done in a setting where the scholars were more at leisure to methodically pursue their work.

The Talmud is literally an encyclopedia of Jewish thought dispensed by learned rabbis over a 1,000-year period from the time of Ezra (about 450 B.C.E.) until the end of the sixth century C.E. It covers a whole range of topics from moral obligations to medicine to superstition and consumes some 34-36 volumes on a library shelf. (See p. 163 for explanation of C.E. and B.C.E.)

The *Synagogue* is a place of meeting for teaching, worship, prayer, and for other kinds of assemblies as well (e.g. charitable fund-raising). Its history goes as far back as the Babylonian exile. The focal point of the synagogue assembly room is an elaborate cabinet which houses the scrolls of the five books of Moses. (A scroll may be as long as ninety feet, painstakingly written out manually and carefully proofread for any errors.) When they are not being used, the scrolls are kept in elaborately decorated coverings, reminiscent of the high-priestly vestments.

At the high point of a synagogue service, a scroll is removed from the "holy ark" cabinet and placed on the lectern, where a cantor musically chants the Scripture reading for the day. Other parts of the service include prayers from a prayer book and a teaching sermon from the rabbi.

Out of reverence for God, Orthodox and Conservative men and boys cover their heads during services with a little round "skull cap" called a *yarmulke* in Yiddish or a *kippah* in Hebrew. Believing that all of life is to be lived with reverence for God, an Orthodox man or boy may wear the kippah all the time. A prayer shawl with fringes (shawl called *tallit*, fringes called *tzitzit*) is worn by Orthodox and Conservative men as a visual reminder of the commandments of the Lord. (See Numbers 15:37-41.) The fringes at each corner of the shawl are symbolically wound together, one long thread wrapped around the other seven threads thirty-nine times, with five knots interspersed. This represents, it is suggested, the thirty-nine books of the Hebrew Scriptures, with the five knots signifying the five books of of the Torah.[5] An Orthodox man regularly wears a vest with fringes underneath his outer clothing, to continually remind himself of God and the Law.

For morning prayers, the observant Jewish man will lay *tefillin* (phylacteries) on his left arm and on his forehead as a literal way of practicing Deuteronomy 6:8: "Tie them as symbols on your hands and bind them on your foreheads." The tefillin are small, leather-covered boxes containing certain Scriptures from Exodus and Deuteronomy handwritten on parchment.[6]

The cubical boxes are attached to leather straps wound around the arm and hand, and the head, in symbolic fashion.[7] The phylactery on the arm represents serving God with one's strength and skill, the left arm being

---

5 The numerical value of the Hebrew letters in tzitzit adds up to 600. Adding the 8 threads and 5 knots makes a sum of 613, the number of commandments in the Law, according to tradition.

6 The Scriptures include these passages: Exodus 13:1-10 and 11-16 and Deuteronomy 6:4-9 and 11:13-21, referring respectively to the exodus deliverance, dedication of the firstborn, God's oneness and his Word, and the promised land.

near the heart, the "center of one's devotion." The phylactery on the head symbolizes committing your mind to
God's service. To the outside doorframe of their house
(and on interior doorframes as well), observant Jews attach
tiny decorated, oblong boxes containing Scripture from the
Shema[8] passages in Deuteronomy 6:4-9 and 11:13-21. Each
of these tiny boxes, called a *mezuzah*, is a reminder of the
constant presence of God.

Keeping kosher (*kashrut*, meaning "fitness") is another
practice of the observant Jewish family. It involves following the lists of edible foods as mentioned in Leviticus 11
and Deuteronomy 14 and ensuring that meat bought is
from an animal that was properly slaughtered according to
the directives of Leviticus 17:10-14. (The animal is to be
killed swiftly and all blood drained from the meat.) The
slaughtering is done by a trained butcher and the meat is
properly approved by an official inspector.

Keeping kosher also means not eating meat and dairy
products together. The very observant have separate dishes and cookware for meats and dairy foods. This comes
from the scriptural commands not to cook a young goat in
its mother's milk.[9] Those commands probably referred to a
pagan practice from which God's people were to disassoci-
ate themselves. But this kosher practice of separating meat
and dairy foods is an example of "putting a fence around
the Torah," making certain that the intent of God's law is
not broken by accident.

---

7 Three Hebrew letters which compose the word *Shaddai*, a name for
God referring to his power, are formed by the way in which knots are
formed in the arm and head straps of the phylacteries and by the way in
which the arm strap is wrapped around the palm of the hand. Additionally,
the long arm strap is wrapped seven times around the forearm and three
times around the middle finger, symbolizing God's betrothal to his covenant
people.

8 Shema is the Hebrew word "Hear!" The command in Deuteronomy
6:4 is, "Hear, O Israel, the Lord our God, the Lord is one."

9 See Exodus 23:19, 34:26 and Deuteronomy 14:21.

Family rituals include circumcision, bar mitzvah and bat mitzvah, and marriage. The circumcision ceremony, performed by a trained and licensed specialist, is performed on the eighth day after birth, affirming the place of male babies in the covenant community. The family praises God, offers a prayer for the infant, and names the child.

At age thirteen, Jewish sons undergo *bar mitzvah*, the "son of the commandment" ceremony. After being carefully prepared for this special occasion, the young man participates in the synagogue in chanting from the Torah. He also puts on tefillin for the first time. Now he is old enough to be counted as one of ten men needed to form a *minyan* in order to hold a public worship service. Reform congregations have developed *bat mitzvah* ceremonies for thirteen-year-old daughters.

The Israel Ministry of Tourism, North America

In Israel, many children celebrate bat mitzvah and bar mitzvah in ceremonies at the Western Wall of Jerusalem.

It is extremely important for the observant Jewish family, especially, that a son or daughter not intermarry with a Gentile. If the fiancé is Gentile, it is expected that he (or she) will undergo instruction to convert to Judaism. The marriage ceremony is generally led by a rabbi under a *huppah* (canopy).[10] Glasses of wine are drunk to represent joy. The marriage contract is read. The bridegroom shatters a glass under his foot to symbolize the seriousness of life in the midst of joy. It may also serve as a reminder of the sorrow experienced at the destruction of the Temple.

A contemporary testimony

A young Jewish dentist who with his veterinarian wife is adopting a Torah-observant lifestyle commented in a newspaper article that traditional, observant Judaism is a way of maintaining something important for them and the next generation. He thought his parents' generation suffered from certain insecurities. He felt secure enough in being here in this country (the U.S.) that he could be both a practicing Jew and feel comfortable as a citizen.

Study questions for reflection and discussion

1. Helpful for further reading is Gordon Jessup's *No Strange God* (London: Olive Press, 1976). The book outlines the practice of Jewish faith and life.

2. Make plans with a local rabbi, if possible, for your church group to visit a synagogue service.

3. How might you approach a religious Jew and a secular Jew differently in a witnessing situation?

4. What traditions do you practice which bring meaning to your faith? Are there other creative traditions which you would like to experiment with to enrich the expression of your faith? When does a tradition become "legalistic"?

---

10 The huppah canopy may represent the home which is being established.

6

Whatever happened to the Messianic Jews?

A day-after-Pentecost story

"Simon! Simon Peter!"

"Why, good morning, Benjamin! How's the good rabbi this morning?"

"Not very good, Simon. But I don't suppose you have time to listen. You seem to be in a hurry."

"Well, I'm off to an early prayer service at the temple. But I always have time for my good friend the rabbi. What's on your mind, Benjamin?"

"Simon, I was there yesterday. I saw the commotion, heard the strange speaking. I listened to your sermon. Simon, you were not yourself. You were absolutely captivating. But do you know what you were preaching, Simon?"

"Yes, Benjamin, I do."

"No, Simon, you don't! If we followed what you said, it would be the end of Judaism. You were announcing the Messianic age! You decried our putting to death that blaspheming heretic Yeshua! You claimed he rose from the dead! You equated him with the coming Messiah and told people to repent and to believe in this impostor! And you topped it off, you and your heretical bunch of Yeshua's disciples, by baptizing 6,000 of that emotionally-charged mob!"

"Benjamin, Benjamin, get hold of yourself! Calm down! It was only 3,000 who received the *mikveh*.[1] But more importantly, we are not doing away with Judaism. I told you I was on my way to the temple. Something new is happening, however. God is bringing fulfillment to Jewish faith. He sent his Son to be the once-for-all sacrifice for sin. He has sent his Spirit to anoint and empower a new Covenant community of his people. This is what the prophets foretold, Benjamin! Oh, I pray you could see what God is doing. I wish you could become a part of it."

"No, Simon, no. Say no more. What I see is that you have become a traitor. We . . . we used to be such good friends. Our wives loved to be together. But . . . but I see that all of that has come to an end. I had hoped, but . . . good-bye, Simon. I shall miss you."

"Benjamin! Don't go away, Benjamin! Benjamin. . . ."

Disappearance of the early Messianic groups

Simon Peter was right! The early New Covenant (New Testament) community *was* clearly Jewish. Its members and leaders were Jewish, its base was the Jewish homeland, and there was a close relationship with the synagogue. The followers of Jesus, known as the people of "The Way," were a part of the Jewish family.

There were several groups in the original Messianic movement. The Ebionites rejected Jesus of Nazareth as a divine Messiah and rejected most of the New Testament except for a revised version of Matthew's Gospel. A second group of Messianics became very assimilated with the surrounding world and lost their Jewishness.

A third group, the Nazarenes, freely embraced their Jewish roots along with embracing Yeshua (Jesus) as Messiah. If this group had continued strong, it would have had significant influence on the emerging church. But it disappeared because these Messianic Jewish believers were

---

1 Hebrew term for ceremonial cleansing

rejected by both mainline Judaism and by the developing Christian church.

The Jewish establishment parted ways with the followers of "The Way" of Messiah. The Messianic Jews were seen as traitors because in response to Jesus' warning, many Nazarene Messianic Jews fled Jerusalem when the Roman armies of General Titus appeared in 70 C.E. (See Luke 21:20-24.) Thus, many of them survived while many other Jews were massacred.

They were also thought to be traitors when they refused to support Bar Kochba's revolt against Rome about 65 years after Titus's assault. Bar Kochba designated himself as the Messiah. The Messianic disciples could not accept that. The ruthless Bar Kochba put many to death. There were theological differences between Messianic believers and other Jews. Judaism could not accept a Messiah who suffered and died. The followers of "The Way" of Messiah, who would receive Gentile converts without circumcision and without keeping other ritual laws, were viewed as a threat by establishment Judaism. The Pharisees, who survived General Titus's destruction of the temple, severely criticized the Nazarene Jews. Some scholars believe that a prayer of cursing of heretics was added to "the eighteen blessings" in the synagogue service about 90 C.E. in order to effectively cut Messianic Jews out of synagogue worship. At times, Judaism's feeling against the Nazarenes reached the level of destructive hatred.

Unfortunately, on the other hand, the increasingly Gentile Christian church was also in conflict with the Messianic believers. Messianic disciples scattered because of persecution, and as they dispersed beyond Jerusalem and Judea, they spread the gospel among Gentiles. By the grace of God, Gentiles were included in the Body of Messiah.

Eventually there were Gentile leaders in the growing and expanding church who ignored the Messianic Jewish beginnings of the church. The Greek language in which the New Testament was written and the Greek background of many new believers in Messiah led to more Greek influence in the church and less influence from her Jewish roots.

It did not stop there. The Gentile wing of the church interpreted the destruction of the temple as God's complete rejection of Israel as a people. The church was seen as God's "new Israel," despite the teaching of Romans 11.[2] Many Christian leaders felt that from then on, God would work only through the church and no longer with Israel as a people. Scriptures about Israel were spiritualized to mean only the "church."

Furthermore, Gentile believers could not understand why Jewish believers would want to maintain Jewish practices. They thought all of the Jewish rituals were abolished when Messiah fulfilled the first covenant.[3] An increasingly negative attitude was developing in the church against the Jewish roots of Christianity. Several centuries after the destruction of Jerusalem the Messianic community had basically disappeared.

Church and state unite

The disappearance of the Messianic Jewish community was a loss to the church. A great change in the church also moved her away from sensitivity to her Jewish origins. Beginning in 312 C.E., Emperor Constantine adopted a positive attitude toward Christianity. It's not clear whether he was ever a genuine believer himself or whether his motives were only political.[4]

---

2 See Romans 11:1, 2a, 11, 12, 25, and 26. These Scriptures promise that God has not forsaken Israel as a people, and that many Jews will yet accept Messiah. God still has Kingdom purposes to fulfill through the Jewish people which will bring rich blessing.

3 Such was the thought of Justin Martyr in his *Dialogue with Trypho the Jew* (second century, C.E.). Translated by Thomas B. Falls, *Saint Justin Martyr—The Fathers of the Church*, Vol. 6 (Washington, D.C.: The Catholic University of America Press, 1948), pp. 182, 183.

4 From Kenneth Scott Latourette, in *A History of Christianity* (New York: Harper and Row, 1975) p. 92.

In the early centuries of her history, the Christian church had suffered much persecution, but Constantine's tolerance and affirmation of Christianity encouraged the state to join with the church.[5] Persecution became much less likely for Christians.

However, persecution had kept the church pure. Only committed believers would risk joining the suffering Christian community. Now it was acceptable to be a Christian. Even more, it was politically expedient to be a Christian if you wanted to be part of the government. The church was being swallowed by the state. Many were "Christian" in name only.

Unbelievers in the church brought with them their prejudices and anti-Jewish attitudes. When Christianity became the state religion, the Messianic movement ("Jewish Christianity") became outlawed. How ironic, when one remembers that the Christ of "Christianity" is really "Messiah"! The Jewish Messiah had become a "Gentile Christ"!

Christian diatribes against Jews

However, it was not only ruthless political leaders nor the rank and file of the people, with their prejudices, that brought a great divide between Christians and Jews. The church fathers, the leaders in the early centuries of the church, were often outspoken against the Jews. Earlier efforts at dialogue with Jewish people gave way to diatribes against the Jews. Bishop Ambrose of the fourth century advocated burning synagogues as a fit reaction to the Jews for rejecting Jesus.

John Chrysostom, a church father of the fourth century, preached eight sermons against the Jews. He was particularly concerned about Judaizing influence in the church. One can admit that he was a "child of his times," but still his rhetoric is harsh and hard to excuse.

---

5 Latourette asserts that Christianity did not become the one state religion under Constantine. He says that happened under later emperors.

Chrysostom called the Jews "the most miserable of all men" (Discourse IV, section 1).

He said to the Jews, "You did slay Christ, you did lift violent hands against the Master, you did spill his precious blood. This is why you have no chance for atonement, excuse, or defense" (Discourse VI, section 2).

He proclaimed, "The Jews will tell you: 'Men waged war on us; men plotted against us.' When they say this, tell them that men would certainly not have waged war against them unless God had permitted it. . . . Is it not obvious that he hated you and turned his back on you once and for all?" (Discourse VI, section 4).

To fellow Christians, Chrysostom admonished, "Have you had enough of the fight against the Jews? . . . The man who does not have enough of loving Christ will never have enough of fighting against those who hate Christ" (Discourse VII, section 1).[6]

It seems that Chrysostom had a change of heart late in life, but the poisonous seeds had already been sown.

The great theologian Augustine encouraged a loving concern for Jewish people, yet at the same time spoke of the Jewish nation as a marked people. Because of their rejection of Christ, God set them aside and appointed them for judgment as an example to others of the severe consequences of rejecting Christ, Augustine proclaimed. Their preservation, Augustine argued, was for the purpose of teaching that message of God's judgment as a warning to Gentiles. Such a theory portrays the Jewish people in a negative light.

Who really killed Messiah?

Not all Jewish people had rejected Jesus. The common people heard him gladly. Although the Jewish leader

6 Passages from the Discourses translated by Paul W. Harkins, *Saint John Chrysostom—The Fathers of the Church*, Vol. 69 (Washington, D.C.: The Catholic University of America Press, 1979), pp. 71, 154, 160, 177.

Nicodemus believed in him, it was often Jewish leaders who opposed Jesus. When John's Gospel speaks about "the *Jews*" being antagonistic to Jesus, it is referring to "Judeans" as opposed to "Galileans." The word for "Judeans" was the same as the word for "Jews." It was the Jewish *leaders* of Judea who were especially critical of Jesus, not *all* Jewish people.

At the time of Jesus' crucifixion, there were Jewish leaders who handed Jesus over to the Romans, and there was a Jewish mob who yelled, "Crucify him!" But they were not *all* of the Jewish leaders—the Sanhedrin which "tried" him was controlled by the Sadducees, who were more in conflict with Jesus than the Pharisees. And the crowd who cried for his death were not *all* of the Jewish people. It was only *one* of the twelve disciples who betrayed him.

Furthermore, it was the Romans who actually crucified Jesus. Jewish people did not crucify anybody. It was the Roman soldiers who put the crown of thorns on his head, spit on him, beat him, and mocked him as a "king." It was a Roman governor who sentenced him to be crucified, even after he was convinced of Jesus' innocence.

Jew *and* Gentile brought Jesus to his death. All of us "were there"; it was the sins of the *whole* world for which Jesus died. In no way can the full responsibility for Jesus' death be placed upon the Jewish people, even though some said, "His death be on us and on our children." Gentiles too must accept responsibility for Jesus' crucifixion.

The Gentile label of Jews as "Christ killers" is a tragic misconception. All of us, Gentile and Jewish, brought Jesus to his death. Yet it is also true that Jesus chose voluntarily to do the will of the Father and to lay down his life for our sake.

The groundwork for anti-Semitism

The groundwork for later, tragic episodes of anti-Semitism was developed even in the midst of Christianity, as we have seen in this chapter. It would burst out in diabolical heights in the Crusades, the Spanish Inquisition, and the horrors of the Holocaust in our own century. The history is painful, but we need to know it, for it helps shape the thinking and living of Jewish people everywhere.

Remembering the suffering and persecution of some of our Christian ancestors helps us empathize with Jewish people, who have a heritage of suffering. Let us humbly acknowledge the reality of suffering which Christians have caused for Jewish people. Let us live in repentance and love.

Recognizing the Jewish roots of the Christian church can help us reflect whether there are ways to celebrate our faith in keeping with those roots. Embracing our Jewish roots can enrich our faith and can help Jewish believers feel at home in our congregations. Remember that Gentile believers are spiritual Jews, children of Abraham by faith, grafted into the Jewish olive tree!

Study questions for reflection and discussion

1. How can the Scriptures help us battle the evil of anti-Semitism and other prejudices?

2. How do the Scriptures help us understand *who* brought Jesus to his death?

3. What are the dangers of unity of church and state?

4. Search your heart for any reflections of anti-Semitism.

7

A History of Hate
The Hamans, Herods, and Hitlers

Hidden hatred

"My high school classmates used to make anti-Semitic comments to me," said a young Jewish mother whom I will call Rachel. "They even scrawled the words, 'You killed Jesus' on the school buildings where I attended."

After becoming a believer in Messiah, Rachel was still hurt by anti-Jewish comments. She was surprised to hear a Christian describe another person as being "stubborn as a Jew." She didn't understand when a Christian used the expression, "Jew them down!" to depict striking a hard bargain. For awhile Rachel stopped attending church.

Upon learning that Rachel was Jewish, some people changed their talk. But the misunderstandings continued.

"How do you handle the knowledge that your ancestors ('relatives') killed Jesus?" her friends have asked. One Easter, she overheard a Christian say, "The Jews did him in," referring to Jesus' crucifixion. Other friends have told Rachel that she's not as pushy, or rich as they expected her to be. When Rachel's mother visited, they wondered why she didn't wear a lot of gold jewelry.

When Rachel, then a believer in Messiah, and her Gentile Christian fiancé were married, some of his relatives refused to attend the wedding because she was Jewish.

Some relatives commented about their newborn baby son, "There's the Jew face." Rachel and her husband wondered what was meant by such comments.

Rachel's experience illustrates the subtle ways that we can unthinkingly portray negative stereotypes of Jewish people. Check your vocabulary. Then note where anti-Jewish attitudes originate.

Satan's hatred

I believe the root of anti-Semitism is Satan's hatred of the Jewish people. Satan is the first and foremost anti-Semite. He knew that God promised to send a Savior for the world and to bless the whole world through the Jewish people. Satan desperately wants to defeat God's purposes. I believe it is Satan who wants to destroy the Jews.

Various leaders of biblical times were instruments of Satan. The Pharaohs of Egypt enslaved God's people and put them to hard labor. A royal decree ordered that Hebrew male babies be killed. However, God saw to it that the future deliverer Moses was rescued by the Pharaoh's daughter and even educated in Pharaoh's house.

In another era, the wicked Haman persuaded King Ahasuerus of Babylon to order that all the Jews be destroyed. The Purim story tells how the Jewish Queen Esther interceded with the king to save her people.

When Jesus was born, King Herod pretended to want to worship him, when in reality he was out to murder this "rival" king. When the Magi did not return to him, he sent out soldiers to slaughter Jewish male babies under the age of two in Bethlehem and its vicinity. But Satan's plan was again thwarted when God sent Joseph, Mary, and the child Jesus to Egypt. The story of Satan's evil design to destroy the Christ child is told symbolically in Revelation 12:1-5. An enormous red dragon was waiting near a pregnant woman, ready to devour her child at birth. However, the newborn child was caught up to safety by God.

Satan frequently tempted the people of Israel to forsake God, and they did not fulfill God's purposes to be a
light to the nations. God had promised blessings to Israel
for faithfulness but also warned of punishments for dis-
obedience with the intent Israel would repent.

> If you do not carefully follow all the words of this
> law, which are written in this book, and do not revere
> this glorious and awesome name—the LORD your
> God—the LORD will send fearful plagues on you and
> your descendants, harsh and prolonged disasters, and
> severe and lingering illnesses. . . . Just as it pleased the
> LORD to make you prosper and increase in number, so
> it will please him to ruin and destroy you. You will be
> uprooted from the land you are entering to possess.
>
> Then the LORD will scatter you among all nations,
> from one end of the earth to the other. There you will
> worship other gods—gods of wood and stone, which
> neither you nor your fathers have known. Among
> those nations you will find no repose, no resting place
> for the sole of your foot. There the LORD will give you
> an anxious mind, eyes weary with longing, and a
> despairing heart. You will live in constant suspense,
> filled with dread both night and day, never sure of
> your life. In the morning you will say, "If only it were
> evening!" and in the evening, "If only it were morn-
> ing!"—because of the terror that will fill your hearts
> and the sights that your eyes will see. (Deuteronomy
> 28:58, 59, 63-67)

God allowed Israel to be judged. The northern nation
of Israel was taken captive by Assyria, and the southern
nation of Judah was taken into exile by Babylonia. Some
say the Jewish people deserve the suffering they have
experienced, because they have been unfaithful to God.
However, this is *never* an excuse for Christians to persecute
or hate Jewish people or to condone such actions by other
people. The Bible says that *all* people have sinned, Jews
and Gentiles.

Tragically, it has often been Gentile Christians who
have persecuted and murdered the Jewish people.

Satan uses these atrocities of Christians against Jews
as a stumbling block to Jewish people's accepting the gos-

pel of Messiah. It is one of the main hindrances that keeps
the light of the gospel from breaking into the hearts of Jewish people.

"As a child I hated the name of Jesus Christ," Rachel
said. "I grew up hearing how most of my mother's family
in Russia and my father's family in Germany had been
killed by Christians." (Likely they considered all Gentiles
to be "Christian.")

A rabbi confronted me with the fact that Christians,
Christian leaders, had persecuted the Jews.

The terror of the Crusades

The Christian Crusades of the Middle Ages (1100-1300
C.E.) brought murderous persecution to Jewish people.
Turkish Muslims ruled Palestine. The Roman church wanted to rescue the "Holy Land" from the "infidel" Muslims.
A preacher named Peter the Hermit stirred up the passions
of the people. Promised guarantees to avoid hell and pur-
gatory lured soldiers to fight in the Crusades. Serfs and
criminals who joined in this religious war were promised
freedom and pardon.

This motley array of knights, soldiers, serfs, and criminals from Europe marched off toward the East and the
"Holy Land." However, religious zealots decided they
need not wait until they arrived in Palestine to fight "infi-
dels" when there were "infidel" Jews living right in Europe. Further, supplies were needed along the way for the
bands of troops. Encouraged by local bishops, the Crusaders ravaged Jewish homes and communities, killing
innocent victims and stealing their possessions for supplies. Although a few very brave souls tried to stop this
outrage, little could be done. Even in Jerusalem, Jewish
people were herded into a synagogue and burned to death.
The cross which emblazoned the shields of the Crusaders,
which was a symbol of Jesus' sacrificial love, tragically
became a feared and ominous symbol for the Jews.

Restrictions and rumors

Throughout the Middle Ages, the Christian Church found various ways to place restrictions on Jewish people in Europe. Some spread false accusations that Jewish people would kill a Christian child and use the blood to make Passover matzo. Apparently the rumor was based on the death of the Egyptians' firstborn sons in the last of the ten plagues. Some Christians in the Middle Ages imagined that Jewish people were murdering Christian children. In England a rumor suggested that a boy had been kidnapped, crucified, and his blood used to make Passover matzo. The king ordered twenty Jews rounded up and tortured until they confessed to the crime. When the boy's body was found with the blood still in its veins and no signs of a crucifixion, it was declared that a miracle had occurred. He was made a saint, and his shrine brought in money for the church. Such rumors went on for a few centuries in Europe, resulting in Gentile mobs pillaging synagogues and killing Jewish citizens.

Even before Hitler's era, Jewish people were sometimes forced to wear distinctive clothing or a conspicuous badge. One writer described it as a "yellow badge of courage."[1] Pope Innocent III (1198-1216) issued a decree to force Jews to wear such a badge. This made it easy for Christians to avoid Jews. On occasion the distinctive badges invited cruelties from hoodlums.

Good Friday and Easter were often dangerous times for Jewish people, when mobs were apt to stage attacks against them. In Toulouse, France, it became a custom for the court to summon a Jewish elder following the Good Friday service and have him given a violent box on the ear as punishment for the sins of the Jewish ancestors. In 1018 C.E. the court's chaplain delivered such a violent blow that the rabbi fell dead.

---

1 Max I. Dimont, author of *Jews, God and History* (New York: Signet Books, 1962) pp. 245, 254.

From 1347-50 the Black Death plague killed at least one-fourth of Europe's population. Because of their good hygiene, the Jewish populace was not so susceptible to the plague as others. Therefore, their suspicious Gentile neighbors blamed the Jews for causing the plague (e.g. accusing them of poisoning wells). The rumors turned vengeful when free-running mobs put many Jews to death.

Jews were forced to live in crowded, unhealthful ghettos in many cities across Europe to keep them out of contact with the Christian population. Ironically, these ghettos helped preserve the Jewish community and their religious practices.

Jewish people were excluded from joining Christian soldiers in battle for the lords of feudal Europe. This meant that Jews could not hold land either, because the feudal lords distributed land as a reward to those who fought.

Excluded from landholding, and also from craftsmen's guilds, Jewish people turned to commerce. Their skills and their ability with languages made them successful in international trade. As prejudice even squeezed them out of commerce, they excelled in the one thing left—moneylending. The church did not permit its members to lend money for interest, deeming it unbiblical, but allowed people to borrow money from the "infidel" Jews. When the Jewish moneylenders became successful in their profession, they were accused of being greedy "Shylocks."

The iniquities of the Inquisition

The "Holy" Inquisition of 15th century Spain and Portugal, which was to rid the church of heretics, became especially vicious in its attacks against Christianized Jewish people known as Marranos, meaning "swine." They were jailed in filthy cells, tortured on cruel racks, and burned to death in "devils' costumes."

After expelling the Moors (Muslim inhabitants) from their land, King Ferdinand and Queen Isabella were coerced into ridding the nation of her Jewish population also. Jews were ordered to convert and be baptized or to leave.

A third of the 150,000-strong Jewish populace "converted" (at least in name); tens of thousands migrated to other parts of Europe, North Africa, and Turkey, leaving behind their property and possessions; and 10,000 perished in death (many of those in suicide). American school children learn that "in 1492, Columbus sailed the ocean blue." They do not learn that also in 1492, the same king and queen who sent out Columbus also sent off (expelled) from Spain her Jewish population. Confiscated Jewish wealth may have helped finance Columbus's expeditions. Spain suffered great loss because of the thousands of talented Jewish professionals who were forced to flee to other lands. Jews frequently fared better under Muslim-led states than under Christian governments.

The punishments of the pogroms

There were organized attacks against Jewish people in Eastern Europe also, in Poland around 1400, and in later years in Russia in the 19th century. (In Poland, it was sometimes outside invaders who attacked Jews and also massacred Poles.) Villages were pillaged and Jewish citizens were murdered in these pogroms which made the Jews scapegoats for the ills of the nations where they lived. Pogroms continued into the early 20th century.

No reforms in the Reformation

Even the Reformation did not bring relief to the persistent anti-Semitism in Europe. Martin Luther at first reached out with kindness to the Jews; when they did not respond to his message, he attacked them severely, especially near the end of his life.[2] (He also reacted to other

---

2 Luther instructed, "Burn their synagogues and schools; what will not burn, bury with earth, that neither stone nor rubbish remain. In like manner break into and destroy their homes." From George H. Stevens, *Strife Between Brothers* (London: Olive Press, 1979), p. 33.

groups at this stage of his life.) Some Lutherans reached out to Jews in subsequent years, and a number of Jews joined the Lutheran Church. Nevertheless, the anti-Jewish sentiments of Luther and the influence he exerted on the Protestant Church undoubtedly helped lay the groundwork for the diabolical "solution" Hitler and his henchmen devised for "the Jewish problem." Hitler claimed Luther as a German hero.

The horrors of the Holocaust

Although Hitler was baptized in the Roman Catholic Church, he was anti-Christian. He did write that he believed he was in accordance with the Almighty Creator in working against the Jews. Nazi Germany portrayed the Jews as the scapegoat for Germany's loss in World War I. Hitler promoted the "Aryan" race and set out to exterminate the Jewish people.

Compounding the horror of the Nazi Holocaust is the fact that it was carried out by officials who were educated professionals and even family men. An extremely sophisticated and systematic death machine carefully filed information on the Jewish victims and herded them towards death camps and gas chambers.

Many others besides Jews were massacred, often in conjunction with alleged crimes. For the Jews, and the Gypsies, and probably others, their only crime was their very existence. Six million Jews, from the very young to the very old, perished in the Holocaust.

The experience of the Holocaust stretched the faith of Jewish men and women to the limit. Some maintained a stoic faith; some became atheistic. For others, faith became a vigorous wrestling match with God.

In his book *Night*, Author Elie Wiesel, a death camp survivor, tells the story of a boy and several men who were hanged at his camp for some trivial allegations. The boy was so emaciated that he simply swung in the breeze, his body too light to tighten the noose around his neck and bring on a quick death. He hung for a long time between life and death, his tongue drooping from his mouth. The Jewish inmates of the camp were forced to gaze on his agony. The question which arose among the Jews was, "Where was God now?" And Elie's answer was that God was there, hanging on that Auschwitz gallows. It seemed that God had removed himself from being God, that he was as helpless as the dying Jewish boy.

I believe God was there, as a suffering God. He suffered with his people as they were tortured and killed. The Holocaust is a *major* stumbling block to Jewish people's consideration of the claims of Messiah and the gospel. Some Christians worked valiantly and at great risk to save Jews from the death camps and were able to rescue some.[3] But many Christians turned the other way and quietly allowed the fiendish endeavors of the Nazi regime to undertake its "final solution."

A resurgence of racism

Racism, including anti-Semitism, is on the rise in the United States today. Christian identity cults are spreading anti-Semitic propaganda which had been popularized in previous generations by people like Henry Ford and Gerald Winrod and by groups like British Israelists. The *Protocols of the Learned Elders of Zion* document, a forgery and a fraud from late in the 19th century, presented the Jews as involved in international conspiracy. Ford and others publicized this fraud. Jews have been accused of being linked with Communism and an international conspiracy to control the world through banking and trade unions.

---

3 The efforts of Corrie ten Boom and her family in rescuing Jewish people are well known. There were many other individuals and groups who also helped. In Denmark, the king, a devout Christian, led a rescue operation which removed all of Denmark's Jewish population (except for 52 who had been deported previously) to safety in Sweden. The whole Danish population, it is reported, including the king, wore the yellow star in solidarity with the Jewish people.

White supremacist Christian groups slander the Jews, calling them the "devil's children," and allege that the true racial descendants of Abraham are "white Anglo-Saxons" of Britain and the United States. (Even Jesus is said not to be Jewish.) Salvation is literally taught to be "by race (the white race), not by grace."

There are various Neo-Nazi and skinhead groups involved in this current white-supremacist and anti-Semitic crusade. They are zealous and militant. The skinheads are anti-Christian but link up with the Ku Klux Klan and with Aryan Nations "Christian" groups. Their shaved heads are a symbol of being prepared for battle.

I believe Satan is stirring up anti-Semitism among Christians. He does not want Christians to witness to Jewish people about Messiah. One pastor who loves Jewish people was labeled "a male prostitute for international Zionism."[4]

A response of love

We cannot react to hate by hating, but this movement of hate needs to be exposed. Christians need to be warned about current anti-Semitism and work together to combat it, as well as reach out to Jewish neighbors with a loving witness for Messiah.

One creative response to anti-Semitism took place in the Midwest United States in 1988. Right-wing extremist groups were blaming Jews for the failure of many farms. Mennonites and Jews planned exchange visits between rural Mennonite farm families and urban Jewish families. The Mennonites learned that their city Jewish friends were a part of the *solution* to the farm-crisis problem. They found the Jewish community to be concerned about peace and interested in alleviating suffering. A Jewish family

---

4 Louis Lapides presented a carefully researched paper on this topic of current anti-Semitism at the 1989 North American Coordinating Committee conference of the Lausanne Consultation for Jewish Evangelism.

recalled afterwards how good it was to make friends with new people, and a Jewish boy wondered whether that could happen with people all over the world.

We sadly acknowledge past and present hatred of Jewish people by Christians. We need to know the history of anti-Semitism. Our Jewish neighbors are keenly aware of it. Having acknowledged that it indeed happened, we must then repudiate such behavior as absolutely wrong for Christians.

In light of the history of anti-Semitism, Messiah calls us to be humble and repentant in our witness with Jewish friends, yet to proceed with loving confidence.

Two stories

"Christ killer!" a gang of boys shouted at little Mike Gold, who had wandered out of the safety of his Jewish neighborhood. They made threatening gestures and yelled at him again and again, "Christ killer! Christ killer!"

With these horrid words pounding in his ears, Mike ran home to the comfort of his mother's arms. He had never heard of Christ before and had no idea of who he was. And so his mother told him about Jesus Christ, who had been crucified many years ago, and how Christians often accuse Jewish people of being the murderers of Christ.

After that traumatic introduction to Christ and to Christians, it's not surprising that Mike matured to adulthood as an atheist. Ironically, as an elderly man, broken and destitute, he frequented a soup kitchen run by Catholic Christians. There he satisfied the hunger of his stomach, but I am afraid the hunger of his soul went unsatisfied.

"Jesus loves you." Little Mitch Triestman's friend smiled as he spoke the words.

Five-year-old Mitch later asked his mother, "Who is Jesus?"

"Why do you want to know?" The tone of her voice revealed her consternation at the question.

"A friend told me that Jesus loves me," Mitch said.

Despite his mother's protests, Mitch started on a search to discover this Jesus who was said to love him. Twelve years later Mitch came to accept Jesus as his Messiah. Today, he works with an outreach ministry and is actively involved in witnessing to his people, telling them that Messiah Jesus loves them too!

Study questions for reflection and discussion

1. Would you like to do some further reading? A helpful little book for a better understanding of this history of hate is *Strife Between Brothers* by George H. Stevens (London: Olive Press, 1979), which I referred to in a footnote.

2. Are there ways in which you personally might be expressing anti-Semitism? Or your church? If so, what steps can you and/or your church take to work against these anti-Jewish attitudes and actions?

3. Does being against anti-Semitism mean that one needs to support everything which the Jewish community or the nation of Israel supports? Explain.

4. With Christians having been involved in so much persecution and murdering of Jewish people, can you understand a large part of the reason why Jesus, the Christian faith, and the cross are huge stumbling blocks for Jewish people? What are some practical, creative, and loving ways in which you and your congregation can respond?

8

Israel

Living in the Land with Justice

Israel at center stage

The land of Israel is again a Jewish homeland. Many Jews from around the world have migrated to Israel. In the aftermath of the Holocaust, Israel constitutes a sense of identity and security for the worldwide Jewish community.

Israel is a focal point of the world community as well. Historically, this land has been at the hub of the world. Hungry for trade and commerce and thirsty for military conquest, the nations of the Middle Eastern and Mediterranean worlds crisscrossed tiny Israel. The people of Israel were dispersed throughout the Middle East and eventually throughout the world. Today, Israel is again a nation. And surrounded by the oil-producing nations of the Middle East, embroiled in conflict with these Arab nations, and entangled with the Palestinians within her borders, Israel is again at center stage of the world.

For many Christians, fulfillment of biblical prophecy focuses on Israel and the Middle East. The rise of modern Israel indicates to them a sign of Messiah's imminent second coming. Other Christians believe the prophecies concerning Israel and the land were fulfilled before Messiah came (in the return of Jewish exiles to the land), or that they are now being fulfilled in the Church as God's people. They are often concerned, however, with the Middle East, emphasizing the need to work for justice for the oppressed and reconciliation for those in conflict.

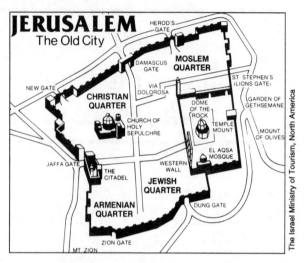

Jewish, Christian, and Muslim peoples look to the land of Israel as a geographical and religious focal point. For Jews and for Palestinian Arabs, Israel is home. This deep fervor for their homeland has led to continuing conflict. Israeli Jews do not all respond the same to their Arab neighbors. Listen to the two perspectives which follow.

Coexistence: two views

"I don't hate Arabs. I think every enlightened man has to fight against the beast in himself. Revenge, for example, and hatred are primitive beasts in us. . . . I believe that if the hatred will disappear, we can exist here with very good relations, because we have a lot in common. We are both Semitic nations. We speak almost the same language. . . . We can live with each other, if we will not compete, if we will not fight. . . . I personally don't believe that there will be real peace until the idea of war as a solution dies" (words of I. Ben Yosef, an Israeli army official).

"Palestine was supposed to be divided into two states, one Arab and one Jewish. The Arab state is now called Jordan. They attacked and were defeated, and they attacked again and again. They obviously don't want us here. . . . Why fight for these few measly rotten kilometers that have nothing but sand and rock? They insist that they want this, and I resent it. The Jewish people have no land that they can call their own, where they can be the majority and make their own decisions, whether for right or for wrong. The Palestinians should have a place too, but it shouldn't have to interfere with the Jewish people who also must have a place. There must be a place, in my opinion, where somebody doesn't say, 'You dirty Jew, go back to where you came from'" (words of Leah Goralsky, a U.S. Zionist immigrant to Israel).[1]

These are the reflections of just two Israeli Jewish persons about whether the Jews and the Palestinian Arabs can live together in the land of Israel. Whose land is Israel? The Jews'? The Palestinian Arabs'? Is it the homeland of both? Does the Bible answer these questions? Do military battles decide the issue? Do a focus on biblical prophecy/promise and a concern for contemporary justice mutually exclude each other? Let us begin to answer these questions by looking at some First Covenant promises concerning the land of Israel.

The land and First Covenant promises

To Abraham, God promised:
I will establish my covenant as an everlasting covenant between me and you and your descendants after you for the generations to come, to be your God and the God of your descendants after you. The

1 Both of these quotes are from *The Israelis—The Portrait of a People in Conflict* by Frank H. Epp (Scottdale, PA: Herald Press, 1980); first one from p. 20, second one from p. 61.

whole land of Canaan, where you are now an alien, I
will give as an everlasting possession to you and your
descendants after you; and I will be their God." (Genesis 17:7, 8)

However, both Ishmael, the father of the Arabs, and
Isaac, the second generation father of the Jews, were sons
of Abraham. Were both peoples promised the land of
Canaan as an everlasting possession? Both sons were
promised to have offspring who would each become a
great nation. (See Genesis 21:13 about Ishmael and Genesis
26:4 about Isaac.) It was to Isaac and his descendants that
the land was particularly promised (Genesis 26:4). In
Jacob's dream, in Genesis 28:13, the promise of the land
was also given for him and his posterity. When God appeared to Moses to call him to be Israel's deliverer from
Egyptian slavery and oppression, he promised to bring the
Israelites out of Egypt to the land of the Canaanites and
other inhabitants—"a land flowing with milk and honey"
(Exodus 3:16, 17).

Was the land promised to Israel forever, with no
strings attached? Were there any conditions for being able
to dwell in the land? Consider these Scriptures:

> See, I set before you today life and prosperity, death
> and destruction. For I command you today to love the
> LORD your God, to walk in his ways, and to keep his
> commands, decrees and laws; then you will live and
> increase, and the LORD your God will bless you in the
> land you are entering to possess. But if your heart
> turns away and you are not obedient, and if you are
> drawn to bow down to other gods and worship them,
> I declare to you this day that you will certainly be
> destroyed. You will not live long in the land you are
> crossing the Jordan to enter and possess. (Deuterono-
> my 30:15-18)[2]

> If you really change your ways and your actions and
> deal with each other justly, if you do not oppress the
> alien, the fatherless or the widow and do not shed

---

2 See also Deuteronomy 11:16-21.

innocent blood in this place, and if you do not follow other gods to your own harm, then I will let you live in this place, in the land I gave your forefathers for ever and ever. (Jeremiah 7:5-7)

The Genesis 17 promise to Abraham about the land was an everlasting covenant made by God. However, God said that Israel would be allowed to continue living in the land only if she was faithful to him. This everlasting covenant is based on the people of Israel acting with justice to those around her. Even so, in the initial conquest of the land, following the exodus from Egypt, God declared that it was *not* because of Israel's righteousness but because of the wickedness of the Canaanite inhabitants that the Canaanites were being ousted and God's people brought in (Deuteronomy 9:4-6).

Israel did suffer exile from the land because of unfaithfulness to God. The Northern Kingdom of Israel was taken captive in 722 B.C.E. by the Assyrians, and Judah, the Southern Kingdom, was exiled in 586 B.C.E. by the Babylonians. Small groups of exiles returned to Palestine at several different times under Zerubbabel, Ezra, and Nehemiah. Some restoration of the land and of Jerusalem occurred.

God promised through his prophets that there would be a restoration of the people of Israel to the land:

The desert and the parched land will be glad; the wilderness will rejoice and blossom. . . . And the ransomed of the Lord will return. They will enter Zion with singing; everlasting joy will crown their heads. (Isaiah 35:1a, b, 10)

"I will bring Judah and Israel back from captivity and will rebuild them as they were before. . . . In the towns of the hill country, of the western foothills and of the Negev, in the territory of Benjamin, in the villages around Jerusalem and in the towns of Judah, flocks will again pass under the hand of the one who counts them," says the LORD. (Jeremiah 33:7, 13)

"For I will take you out of the nations; I will gather you from all the countries and bring you back into your own land. I will sprinkle clean water on you, and you will be clean; I will cleanse you from all your impurities and from all your idols. I will give you a new heart and put a new spirit in you; I will remove from you your heart of stone and give you a heart of flesh. And I will put my Spirit in you and move you to follow my decrees and be careful to keep my laws. You will live in the land I gave your forefathers; you will be my people, and I will be your God. . . . This is what the Sovereign LORD says: On the day I cleanse you from all your sins, I will resettle your towns, and the ruins will be rebuilt." (Ezekiel 36:24-28, 33)

"I will bring back my exiled people Israel; they will rebuild the ruined cities and live in them. They will plant vineyards and drink their wine; they will make gardens and eat their fruit. I will plant Israel in their own land, never again to be uprooted from the land I have given them," says the LORD your God. (Amos 9:14, 15)

This is what the LORD Almighty says: "Once again men and women of ripe old age will sit in the streets of Jerusalem, each with cane in hand because of his age. The city streets will be filled with boys and girls playing there. . . . It may seem marvelous to the remnant of this people at that time, but will it seem marvelous to me?" declares the LORD Almighty. . . . "I will bring them back to live in Jerusalem; they will be my people, and I will be faithful and righteous to them as their God." (Zechariah: 8:4, 5, 6b, 8)

It is difficult to simply dismiss the prophets' references to the land and the people of Israel being resettled there. These passages appear to refer to a more general restoration than happened following the exile. However, they also show God speaking not only about a renewal of the land but about a renewal of the heart as well. Even if modern Israel is seen by some as a fulfillment of these prophecies, one needs to admit that spiritual restoration has happened to only a minority of the people. One can anticipate a more general revival occurring at a future time.

I ask then: Did God reject his people? By no means! I am an Israelite myself, a descendant of Abraham, from the tribe of Benjamin.... But if their transgression means riches for the world, and their loss means riches for the Gentiles, how much greater riches will their fullness bring! . . . For if their rejection is the reconciliation of the world, what will their acceptance be but life from the dead? . . . And so all Israel will be saved, as it is written: "The deliverer will come from Zion; he will turn godlessness away from Jacob. And this is my covenant with them when I take away their sins." (Romans 11:1, 12, 15, 26, 27)

Some students of the Bible say that the messages of the prophets about restoration to the land refer to God's creating a new people of God, the Church.[3] Although the people of God transcends all geographical boundaries, might it be that God also includes the geographical land of Israel in his promises spoken through the prophets? Before 1948, it was much easier to say that the real estate of Israel (or Palestine) was not significant in God's plans. It is not quite so easy to make that assumption now. That is not to say that all Bible students see Israel today as even a partial fulfilling of prophecy. Nor does it mean, even if one assumes that contemporary Israel is pertinent to biblical prophecy, that God's hand and will are in everything that has happened in the establishment of the nation of Israel, or in every action taken by the government of Israel. I will say more about that later.

---

3 Or, the restoration is seen as fulfilled in the return after the exile. Romans 11 indicates that God has not replaced the people of Israel with the Church in his kingdom purposes (Romans 11:1, 11-15). Gentile believers have been "grafted into" the Jewish roots of the people of God (Romans 11:17-21). God intends to bless the whole people of God through a coming Jewish renewal (Romans 11:12, 15). Fred Klett (Chaim Ministries, Presbyterian Church in America) suggests that God has *expanded* his kingdom purposes beyond ethnic Israel, through the Church. (This is different from saying that Israel has been replaced by the Church.) He also suggests that the present-day restoration of the nation of Israel may be a providential preparation by God for the Messianic revival, as well as God's continuing preservation of the Jewish people.

The land and the New Covenant context

Is it not significant that Messiah's life and ministry occurred in the land of Israel? He was born in Bethlehem. He grew up in Nazareth. He did the majority of his teaching and miracles within the land. He died on a hill outside Jerusalem. He ascended to his heavenly Father from a spot near the village of Bethany.

It was in Jerusalem that God poured out the Holy Spirit, and a great many people turned to the Lord after Peter's Spirit-empowered sermon on the day of Pentecost. The Church, God's New Covenant people (who at first were all Messianic Jewish people) was established in Jerusalem, Judea. Later the Church reached out to Samaria and then to Antioch and many other places, as the scattered believers did evangelism and church planting. But for some time, Jerusalem continued to be the "mother church." The great conference about how to integrate Gentile believers into the church was held at Jerusalem. Paul gathered relief offerings to send back to the suffering mother church. Jerusalem was either a starting or ending point, or both, for three of Paul's missionary trips.

The culmination of all things in the end time, described in Revelation 21, pictures God's people eternally dwelling with God in the heavenly age as "the Holy City, the new Jerusalem." Thus the image of Zion, the capital city of the land of Israel (or Judah), set on a hill, is used to describe the eternally redeemed people of God.

We do need to remember, however, that God's people are now his temple, not a sanctuary in Jerusalem. One of the things that got Stephen in trouble in his Acts 7 sermon to the Sanhedrin (Jewish ruling body) was his statement to them that God does not live in a house made by human hands (Acts 7:48-50).[4]

---

4 The New Testament does not expressly affirm the promise of the land to Israel (except for the reference to "the promises" in Romans 9:4). On the other hand, it is also true that neither does the New Testament explicitly say that the promises of the land are done away with.

Diaspora, Zionism, and "making alijah"[5]

We looked at the dispersion and exile of the Jewish people from the land of Israel. We have seen the terrible history of hatred and persecution brought against the Jews who were dispersed throughout the world. The Jewish people are still mostly living in the diaspora, this dispersion among the nations. Only four and a half million or so of the fourteen million-plus worldwide population of Jewish people live in Israel.

At the end of the 19th century, the diaspora began to be reversed. Theodore Herzl, the father of Zionism (which called for the establishment of a homeland for the Jews), convened the first Worldwide Zionist Conference in Basel, Switzerland, in 1897. He felt the answer to anti-Semitism was to have a Jewish homeland and prophesied that in fifty years there would be a Jewish state. In 1917, Great Britain adopted the Balfour Declaration that Palestine should be a homeland for the Jews, and British General Allenby marched into Jerusalem, capturing it from the Turks without firing a shot.

The League of Nations placed Palestine under Great Britain's trust as a mandate nation. Much of it was turned into the Arab kingdom of Jordan, with a small portion named Palestine reserved for the Jews. Jews slowly migrated to Palestine, with increasing numbers moving there as Hitler's regime began escalating its anti-Jewish program. After World War II, despite great Arab pressure, the United Nations voted on November 19, 1947 (fifty years after Herzl's prediction), to partition Palestine into a Jewish state and an Arab state. The United States supported the U.N. vote but some time later urged the U.N. to abolish the partition. However, when the British left Palestine, on May 14, 1948, the Zionist General Council announced yet that day the establishment of the state of Israel, and 75 minutes

---

5 To "make *alijah*" means to "become an Israeli citizen."

later, President Truman astounded the world by declaring
the U.S. recognition of Israel.

Israel fought four wars in twenty-five years against
the Arabs (one for independence in 1948-49, against the
Arab League; one against Egypt in 1956; the Six Day War
in 1967, in which Israel seized Arab land and unified
Jerusalem; and the Yom Kippur War in 1973). The Arabs
had left the U.N. debate in 1947, crying, "Perish Judea!"
They vowed to push the Jews into the sea. Yet Israel won
each of the four military conflicts and managed to survive
as a state. Not all Jews have supported Zionism and the
establishment of the state of Israel. Some of the Orthodox
believe that only Messiah can set up a Jewish homeland.
One Orthodox sect in Israel was fined by the Israeli government for making a contribution in foreign currency to a
Palestinian hospital. However, Jews from around the world,
even from distant places like Shanghai, have come to Israel
to "make alijah." It is also true that many Jews have emi-
grated *from* Israel. For some, the difficulties of adjusting to
the land (uncertain economy, waiting two years to acquire
a telephone, etc.) outweigh the joys of being in *Eretz Israel*
(the land of Israel).

Whose land?

The Palestinian Arab and Israeli Jewish conflict continues, adding to the difficulty and uncertainty of living in
Israel. How should the Palestinian question be resolved?
Does the 4,000-year-old biblical promise of the land to
Abraham and recent military victories take precedence
over the right of a homeland for Palestinians, who have
also lived in the land for hundreds of years?

In his book *Blood Brothers*, Elias Chacour, a Palestinian
Melkite Christian, tells the story of their village in northern
Galilee being evacuated and later destroyed by Israeli sol-
diers when he was a boy. Elias's father always counseled a
non-retaliatory response to the aggressors. As an adult,
Elias has worked hard at going beyond passive non-retali-

ation to being an aggressive peacemaker. He is a spokesman for reconciliation between Palestinians and Jews and has helped organize efforts to work at peace.

Elias points out that even Abraham, the recipient of God's promise concerning the land, lived as a nomad who dealt justice towards others who also lived in the land. He accepts the fact that the Jews have returned in large numbers to the land of promise, but he states that God calls his people to live in the land with justice to the foreigner (the Palestinian). (See Isaiah 56:1-8.) Elias does not side with Palestinian terrorists. He proposes a third way, neither violence nor passively giving in, but actively working at peacemaking and reconciliation. He deplores those who quickly assume that Israel's presence in the land is the fulfillment to end time prophecy and who popularize interpretations of prophecy with announcements that the second coming of Christ is about to happen.[6]

Elias cautions that this is an incomplete understanding of prophecy. It deals only with events being fulfilled and neglects to ask whether righteousness and justice are being fulfilled. I affirm that the establishment of a Jewish homeland of Israel is right and appropriate and that this may be a prelude to God's drawing many, many Jews to turn to him. However, one can ask whether this needs to mean violent conflicts and bloody wars. The Hebrew prophets speaking for God called their people to live in the land with justice for all of the inhabitants of the land.[7]

Many in the Israeli government, of course, do not profess to follow the way of God and the way of Messiah. Israel is basically a secular state. There are small groups of Israelis working for peaceful relations with Palestinian

---

6 Chacour suggests in his book *Blood Brothers* (Chosen Books, Revell Co., 1984), pp. 140-141, that the return of Jews to Israel and the establishment of a Jewish homeland is a sign of God to the nations that he is a holy Lord and that he leads a holy people—desiring for Israel to live righteously.

7 See also Isaiah 56:6-8, Jeremiah 7:6,7, and Leviticus 19:18.

neighbors, but can one expect secular Israel to live according to God's way of justice and peacemaking?

A biblical and godly model is Isaac, who lived peaceably with those who confiscated his wells. (See Genesis 26:12-24.) He moved on until God "made room for him." God is the one who takes vengeance on evil. We are to leave vengeance with him. It may well be that God will only allow the Jews to "have room" in Israel if they "make room" for their Palestinian Arab neighbors within their borders.

There are models of peacemaking in Israel within the Messianic/Christian context. There are people like Elias Chacour working for peace. There is a congregation like Beit Immanuel where Jewish and Arab believers in Messiah fellowship together, presenting a powerful demonstration that *Messiah* can bring peace, uniting in his body Jews and Arabs, breaking down the wall of hostility. In Messiah, reconciliation is possible!

Israel's future: one view

What is the future of Israel? How does it fit into God's completion of human history on earth? One view sees the end of history initiated as Christ comes back for the Church. Then the nations of the world, influenced by the evil antichrist, come against the nation of Israel. These nations are thought to include the area of Russia from the north, Egypt from the south, and China from the east, among others. This battle is referred to as "Armageddon." Israel will have a spiritual revelation of Messiah, the pierced one. Two-thirds of Israel will be struck down. But there will be a time of great spiritual refining and revival in the midst of great tribulation for Israel. Gentiles will experience tribulation also. Messiah will reappear, standing on the Mount of Olives and splitting it in two through natural cataclysmic events and by the power of his word. He will defeat the nations who are making war against Israel and establish a worldwide kingdom of peace, with Jerusalem as its capital. The survivors of the nations who were attacking Israel will come up to Jerusalem to celebrate the Feast of Tabernacles and to worship the King of kings. The temple in Jerusalem will be standing again, for memorial sacrifices. At the end of one thousand years, all people will be judged, the unrighteous sent to eternal separation from God in hell and the righteous gathered into the eternal presence of God and Messiah.[8]

Israel's future: an alternative view

An alternative view of end time events interprets the Scriptures referred to in the preceding footnote more symbolically than literally. Or, another way of putting that is to say that a detailed timeline of end time events is not pulled from these and other scriptural passages. Rather, overall themes are outlined: a time of encroaching evil, a revival among Jewish people with a majority turning to faith in Messiah as he shows himself to them, evil overthrown by the sovereign Messiah who rules as King of kings, the unrighteous sent to eternal hell and the righteous invited into God's eternal, heavenly kingdom.

Messiah will reign eternally, and in the process of his culminating world history, he will draw many, many Jews to faith in him. (See Romans 11:12, 15, 26.)

Study questions for reflection and discussion

1. How significant do you think the place of Israel is in relation to end time events? (Consider that God has preserved Israel as a people for these thousands of years.)

2. Is there a danger in overemphasizing the fulfillment of prophecy in Israel today, to the neglect of a concern for justice and righteousness? What is a godly response to oppression and terrorism?

---

8 For scriptural study, see Ezekiel 37 and 38 (also chapters 39-48), Daniel 11, Zechariah 12—14, and Revelation 19:11—21:8.

3. How could an understanding of end time prophecy be helpful in witnessing for Messiah to Jewish people? How might one use the facts of God's preservation of the Jewish people and of the restoration of Jewish people to the land of Israel in witnessing to Jewish people?

4. Do you believe God is working through the nation of Israel today in a unique way, different from his working through other nations? Consider that God's kingdom is supra-national (above the nations) and that the people of God through Messiah is multi-national. What implications does all of this have for the Church, the worldwide Body of Christ?

5. Do you believe God yet has special purposes to work out for the Church and the world through a great spiritual awakening and turning of Jewish people to God, through Messiah? What implications would that have for witness to Jewish people?

6. Some resources for further reading and study, from different perspectives, are: *Blood Brothers*, by Elias Chacour, with David Hazard (Chosen Books—Revell Co., 1984); *The Message of Revelation*, by Michael Wilcock (Intervarsity Press, 1975) in which pages 175-182 have a discussion of several millenial views; *View the Land*, by Anne Dexter (Bridge Publishing, 1986) which generally follows the first view about Israel's future which I briefly summarized above.

9

The Messianic Jewish Movement
What is it?

Jewish and *Christian?*

Can one be Jewish and Christian at the same time?

"Yes," says David Chansky, who has been leader of the Ohev Yisrael congregation near Washington, D.C. Being Jewish and affirming faith in Messiah Jesus do belong together.

At one time in his life, he would not have thought so. When David came to faith in Messiah, well-meaning Christians told him he would need to give up his Jewishness. For years he believed them. Sadly he put aside his prayer shawl and phylacteries. He no longer celebrated Jewish holidays, but he really missed Rosh Hashanah, Yom Kippur, and Passover.

However, David came to realize that Messiah Jesus had practiced his Jewishness. Jesus went to synagogue and celebrated the festivals. "Rabbi Saul" wrote that the "cultivated olive tree," the God-fearing Jews, sustained the real root of faith and that Gentile believers in Messiah were like wild olive shoots grafted into the main trunk and the roots of the Jewish "family tree." David recognized how Jewish early followers of Yeshua (Jesus) had been.

David Chansky visited a Messianic congregation and later planted a new one. At Ohev Yisrael, the God of Israel is worshiped through a personal relationship with his Son, Messiah Jesus. The atmosphere of Ohev Yisrael is very Jewish. Men wear yarmulkas on their heads. Many of the prayers the people chant are the same as those prayed in the synagogue. A cantor assists in leadership of the congregation and its worship. Most people "keep kosher," but it is not required.[1]

Not a new thing

We have already seen in earlier chapters that Messianic Judaism is not a new thing. The early church of the book of Acts was at first made up only of Messianic Jews, Jews who professed faith in Jesus as the Messiah. Paul practiced a Messianic Jewish faith. He had Timothy, born of a Greek-Jewish marriage, circumcised for the sake of Jews in that area of Asia Minor (Acts 16:3). He joined in purification rites with a group of Jewish men in Jerusalem, in order to allay criticism that he was teaching Jewish believers in Messiah to forsake their Jewish customs (Acts 21:17-26). He announced in Rome that he had done nothing against his people or the customs of their Jewish ancestors (Acts 28:17). He lived like a Jew, he said, because he wanted to win Jewish people to faith in Messiah (1 Corinthians 9:20). Paul, the apostle to the Gentiles, also had a priority of ministering to his own Jewish people!

The early Messianic Jewish community, rejected by non-Messianic Jews as well as by the increasingly Gentile Christian church, gradually disappeared. It was gone by the fourth century. For many hundreds of years, there were no Messianic Jewish congregations.

A resurrection of Messianic Judaism

In the early 20th century, Messianic congregations began to arise again. In the late 19th century, Rabbi Isaac

---

1 David Chansky's story is told in *Jesus for Jews*, edited by Ruth Rosen (San Francisco: A Messianic Jewish Perspective, 1987), pp. 242, 272.

Lichtenstein of Hungary led the first Messianic congregation in over 1,400 years. Early in his rabbinic service, he
had found a New Testament in one of his district schools
and in anger had tossed it onto one of his library shelves.
Some 30 years later, in researching why Christians were
rising up in anti-Semitism, he came across this New Testament. As he read it, he became convinced that Jesus was
indeed the Messiah.

For three years Rabbi Lichtenstein kept quiet about
his belief. Then he began to use New Testament Scriptures
in his synagogue preaching. His listeners were astonished.
One Sabbath he openly announced that he was using the
New Testament and that he believed Jesus was Israel's
Messiah and Redeemer. He wrote pamphlets about his
beliefs and urged his congregational members to believe in
Messiah Jesus.

Jews throughout Hungary and Central Europe were
amazed. Rabbis were incensed. Rabbi Lichtenstein was
called before the chief rabbi in Budapest, but he refused to
recant. He did not become silent nor leave his rabbinical
post. His congregation supported their rabbi despite the
pressure they experienced. Eventually, he did resign his
position as a district head rabbi and took to a writing ministry, exhorting his people with the message from Hosea
14:1, "Return, O Israel, to the LORD your God."[2]

Joseph Rabinowitz was another Jewish believer in
Messiah who headed up a Messianic congregation in Hungary. Hebrew-Christian alliances were developing since
the mid-19th century in Great Britain, and since 1925 in
America. The International Hebrew Christian Alliance
began in 1925. In the 1920s and 1930s, a few Messianic Jewish (or Hebrew Christian) congregations emerged in the
United States. Some Christians criticized this movement,
believing that a wall was being re-erected between Jewish

---

2 Rabbi Lichtenstein's story is told in Louis Goldberg's book, *Our Jewish
Friends* (Neptune, NJ: Loizeaux Brothers, 1977), pp. 171-173.

and Gentile believers in Messiah. Messianic Jews would say they are *tearing down* a 1,500-year-old wall which a Gentilized church built to separate itself from its Jewish roots.

Messianic Jewish congregations have continued to emerge and to grow. There have been growing pains as the congregations develop theology and worship. Congregations continue to change as they work at understanding the biblical and New Covenant meaning of Messianic Judaism.

In the United States today there are over 100 congregations which uphold Messiah Jesus while at the same time maintaining a Jewish context and cultural heritage. These congregations are affiliated with several different organizational bodies. In Israel today there are about thirty Messianic Jewish congregations and home fellowships.

Why Messianic congregations?

First of all, Messianic congregations keep alive the Jewish roots of faith in Messiah Jesus. Messianic Jews have wonderful opportunities to practice their faith in a Jewish context. The Messianic Jewish movement vividly demonstrates the vitality and presence of the faithful Jewish remnant. Paul wrote about this "remnant chosen by grace" in Romans 11:1-6:

> I ask then: Did God reject his people? By no means! I am an Israelite myself, a descendant of Abraham, from the tribe of Benjamin. God did not reject this people, whom he foreknew. Don't you know what the Scripture says in the passage about Elijah—how he appealed to God against Israel: "Lord, they have killed your prophets and torn down your altars; I am the only one left, and they are trying to kill me"? And what was God's answer to him? "I have reserved for myself seven thousand who have not bowed the knee to Baal." So too, at the present time there is a remnant chosen by grace. And if by grace, then it is no longer by works; if it were, grace would no longer be grace.

By choosing not to be assimilated into a Gentile church, Jews in Messianic congregations give a testimony that the faithful remnant exists and that they continue to be God's covenant people. They foreshadow the great Messianic revival prophesied in Romans 11 in which many, many Jewish people will come to faith in Messiah Jesus. They are the firstfruits of that revival.

Second, Messianic congregations maintain a connection to the larger Jewish community. Members of these congregations do not reject their Jewishness; if anything, their Jewishness is enhanced. The planting of Messianic Jewish congregations is an effective means of reaching out with the gospel. Jewish persons visiting a Messianic Jewish congregation have witnessed to the powerful atmosphere of love in the group.

Third, Messianic congregations are a challenge to the larger Christian community to affirm the Jewish roots and heritage of our faith. The natural root and branches—Jewish believers—cannot be ignored. (See Romans 11:16-18.) Acknowledging Messianic Jewish believers as brothers and sisters in the faith also challenges the Gentile church to make witnessing to Jewish people about Messiah Jesus an important priority. "The gospel . . . is the power of God for the salvation of everyone who believes: first for the Jew, then for the Gentile" (Romans 1:16).

Messianic worship and congregational life

Messianic Jewish congregations may hold services on Friday evenings, Saturdays, and/or Sunday mornings. Friday evening and Saturday services keep alive the Sabbath day of rest and worship commanded in the First Covenant. Sunday observance remembers the resurrection of Yeshua on the eighth day/first day and also the pouring out of the Holy Spirit on that day at Shavuot (Pentecost). God was bringing in the New Covenant to fulfill the First Covenant. The Messianic Jewish family celebrates Saturday as a day of rest. The weekly Sabbath celebration renews one's covenant with God and finds added meaning in the spiritual rest which Messiah brings. The family enjoys the special time of being with one another in the Friday evening Sabbath meal. It appears that the early church in Acts worshiped in public services primarily on the Sabbath, not on the first day of the week.

The style of worship in Messianic services is Jewish, yet Yeshua is always central. Prayers similar to the synagogue may be used, but mature Messianic congregations are careful that these prayers express New Covenant theology. Music may be adaptations of Christian hymns or genuinely Jewish music with Messianic themes. To many people, musician Stuart Dauerman and The Liberated Wailing Wall, a Jews for Jesus singing group, are synonymous with the term, "Messianic music." Dancing in joy to the Lord is often integrated into Messianic services. Public reading of Scripture, reciting of the Shema ("Hear, O Israel, the Lord our God, the Lord is one."), with an understanding of its fulfillment in Yeshua, and a teaching sermon are important elements of Messianic worship services.

Messianic Jews celebrate the biblical festivals as significant events in the worship year. Jesus in his life and ministry brought fulfillment to these festivals; they have a prophetic dimension of witnessing to the nations of the world. Celebrating the festivals is an important part of maintaining contact with the Jewish community at large. A young Messianic Jewish mother told me she finds it crucial to continue celebrating Jewish festival times with her non-Messianic parents and family.

Messianic Jewish men may wear a prayer shawl with fringes, phylacteries, and/or a yarmulka. Messianic Jewish families often attach mezuzahs to the doorframes of their homes. In general, Messianic believers are free to practice or not to practice these observances. If practiced, it is the meaning of the principles behind the symbols that is seen as more important than the observances themselves.

Prayer shawl

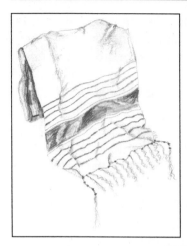

Yarmulke

Phylactery

Maria Leaman

When a baby boy is born into a Messianic Jewish family, circumcision is performed on the eighth day as a general practice. Even if a Messianic Jew emphasizes the fulfillment of the Law of Moses and says that the 613 Jewish laws cannot be binding now that Messiah has come, he or she would still probably acknowledge the special significance of circumcision, because it was a part of God's covenant with Abraham even before the time of Moses. Bar mitzvah and bat mitzvah ceremonies, welcoming 13-year-old boys and girls as adults in the community, are often part of Messianic congregational life.

"Keeping kosher" in Messianic Jewish homes is observed according to individual conviction. David Chansky writes, "If you asked, you would discover that most of our people keep kosher kitchens, though those who don't

are not looked down upon. Above all, you would find the
message that no matter what is eaten or not eaten, whatever is worn or not worn and whichever liturgy is used;
regardless of culture, tradition or style, it is Y'shua, and
Y'shua alone, who can make our hearts truly kosher".[3]

Messianic theology

Obviously, one cannot do justice to this topic in a
short overview. Nor is there a uniform understanding or
interpretation of what the theology of Messianic Judaism
is. Let me outline a brief summary, nonetheless:

1. The Bible is the authoritative word of God. The
   First Covenant ("Old Testament") presents a fore-
   shadowing of the New Covenant ("New Testament"). The New Covenant is a fulfillment of the
   First Covenant. The Bible is the authoritative basis
   of our faith in God through Yeshua and what it
   means to live as a disciple/follower of Messiah.

2. Salvation is by the grace of God through faith in
   Yeshua. Salvation is not by keeping the Law, which
   was impossible to do anyway.

3. The Spirit of God brings life, gives Messianic believers the power to live out the will of God, and
   brings forgiveness when there is repentance after
   failure.

4. Yeshua of Nazareth is God's Messiah (anointed
   Messenger and Deliverer), and Messiah is divine.

5. Messianic congregations provide a biblical, New
   Covenant means of celebrating life in the body of
   Messiah. The Jewishness of biblical faith, of Yeshua,
   and of the early church is affirmed. The community
   of believers is emphasized, including Gentile

---

3 The quote is from *Jesus for Jews*, p. 242. (See footnote earlier in this chapter.) *Y'shua* is another way to spell *Yeshua*.

believers who wish to identify with a Messianic Jewish congregation.

6. There is freedom to keep First Covenant laws so long as they do not conflict with the New Covenant teaching of freedom in Yeshua. Some congregations give more emphasis to keeping the Law of Moses as a part of the Messianic New Covenant. Others emphasize more the freedom "to keep or not to keep" the various practices, because of the freedom of the Spirit and salvation by grace.

7. Witnessing about Messiah to the Jew first and also to the Gentile is a high priority. Services and festival celebrations are often planned with a goal of extending an invitation to unbelievers to turn from sin and place faith in Messiah. There are also witnessing events which take Messianic believers out on the streets or over the airwaves to present the gospel.

8. There is an emphasis that God still keeps his covenant with the faithful remnant of Israel (Messianic Jews), and that God yet has a plan for the whole nation of Israel as well when "all Israel will be saved." The promise of "the land" to the nation of Israel is seen as a part of God's continuing to work out his plan. It is believed that those who curse Israel (faithful remnant and nation as a whole) will be cursed, and that those who bless her will be blessed by God.

9. When Yeshua appears again, it is generally believed he will establish the Messianic kingdom in fullness and rule as king, having defeated the Gentile nations, and that he will bring Israel as a whole to faith in him.

Our response

The Messianic movement is a dynamic movement. It is young and growing, and changing as it matures. It deserves patience and understanding from the larger church. Messianic congregations bring a challenge and blessing to the total body of Messiah.

Visit a Messianic congregation if you can. Anticipate a worship service full of love for Yeshua, joyful praise, and enthusiasm for evangelism. Praise God for the many Jewish people who are discovering Yeshua as Messiah and Savior and in the process often discovering their Jewish heritage as well. It appears that more Jewish people have come to faith in Jesus in the last fifteen to twenty years than in any such time period since the first century. Thank God for the many Messianic Jewish congregations who are witnessing for Messiah and welcoming Jewish and Gentile Messianic believers into the fellowship of God's people.

Study questions for reflection and discussion

1. What are the positive values of Messianic Jewish congregations?

2. Do you see any reasons for caution in the Messianic Jewish movement?

3. Is there a Messianic Jewish congregation near you? If so, make plans to visit a service there.

4. In looking ahead to the next chapter, reflect on that which Jews and Christians hold in common. You might list the things which come to mind.

10

The Things We Have in Common

Getting to know one another

"Do you suppose that could happen with people all over the world?" A Jewish family asked that question as they reflected about visits which took place in 1988 between Kansas City Jewish families and Mennonite Christian farm families, which I referred to earlier.

Right-wing groups in the midwestern U.S. were blaming Jewish people for the failure of farms. In response, Mennonite Central Committee representatives and the Kansas City Jewish Community Relations Bureau set up exchange visits. Jewish families visited Mennonite farm families in rural Kansas. In return, urban Jewish families hosted their rural Mennonite friends in Kansas City. They asked each other: What does it mean to be Mennonite? To be Jewish? And what do we have in common? They discussed the farm crisis, and the Mennonite families discovered their Jewish friends had been actively involved in trying to solve the crisis.

In Kansas City, the Mennonite families participated in Sabbath celebrations: the Friday evening Shabbat meal in a Jewish home, a Saturday morning synagogue service including a bar mitzvah, and a Saturday afternoon Havdalah service concluding the Shabbat. They enjoyed Israeli dancing and saw Jewish points of interest. On Sunday the Mennonite and Jewish friends shared in a morning service at a Mennonite church and later met at the synagogue, looking at the farm crisis, the need to work together with compassion in times of crisis, and issues of anti-Semitism.

The good-byes at the end of the weekend were unhurried. New friendships had developed. The Mennonite families enjoyed the way their Jewish friends had told them their story. They had also discovered that issues of justice and social concern were important to their urban Jewish friends just as they were to them. A Jewish family recalled their earlier farm visit and remarked how good it was to make friends with people they had not previously known.

Hearing one another

In 1984 in eastern Pennsylvania, a group of Jewish and Christian folks had a different kind of meeting. Jewish and Christian scholars and other interested persons met for a day to listen to one another on the central theme of "covenant." Four Jewish scholars and four Christian scholars paired up to give their views on four subtopics as they relate to covenant: salvation, Messiah, land, and community. Those attending heard Jewish scholars speak for themselves and Christian scholars likewise, rather than hearing fellow Jews explain what Christians believe or fellow Christians speak about what Jews believe.

At that consultation, the participants discovered these four topics were important themes that both Jews and Christians consider to be significant and could dialogue about. There were points of commonality in thinking about the theme of Messiah. Both the First Covenant Scriptures and the New Covenant Scriptures speak of Messiah, anticipate a Messianic era, and look for shalom to accompany Messiah. Messiah embodies hope.

Community is important to both Jews and Christians. The concept of community is based on a covenant between God and his people. The faith of the Jewish people and of

Dancing at the Feast of Tabernacles or Booths, which is largely an outdoor celebration

Christian people calls each group to share in community. There is a bond within the community not found in relationships with the larger world. I believe that for groups of Christians who take seriously a life of faithful discipleship, there is a further bond with the Jewish community, especially with the observant (religiously practicing) Jewish community. The Jewish community finds itself to be a minority in the world at large. The radically faithful evangelical Christian community experiences that also.

Christians involved in this 1984 consultation identified areas where Jews were often more faithful than Gentile Christians of the Western world during the heyday of triumphalistic Christendom in reflecting the character and teaching of Jesus. Consider the following characteristics (observed by this consultation) exhibited by many Jewish people in the diaspora but often betrayed by Christendom:

1. True spirituality involves not only the heavenly but also effects a transforming of things on earth.

2. Abhorring violence as a way of trying to right wrongs and being willing to suffer for righteousness' sake are God's way.

3. Salvation is not just an individual matter but is lived out within the community of God's people.

4. The kingdom of God and God's faithful minority cannot identify itself with any particular national state.

5. Affirming peoplehood and community means that hierarchical power will be rejected.

6. The ethics of Jesus' Sermon on the Mount are to be affirmed.[1]

Of course, there are also differences of faith which separate Jews and Christians. There needs to be proclamation beyond dialogue.

Is there a place for dialogue?

At the 1986 Lausanne Consultation for Jewish Evangelism conference held in England, Gerald Anderson of Overseas Ministries Studies Center commented that most evangelical Christians are paralyzed about dialoguing with Jews and that most mainline Christians are paralyzed about proclaiming the gospel to Jews. Anderson asserted that both are appropriate and necessary. Some Christians would maintain that simply dialoguing about each other's faith is the only evangelism that Christians are called to do with Jews. Talk about issues you are both concerned with, talk about your faith and explain what you believe, but do not try to persuade the other to believe as you do, they would say.

However, dialogue can be used in a good way. It is a way of learning, in humility, recognizing that the other

---

1 Adapted from *Mennonite Witness as it Relates To Jewish People*, a statement in pamphlet form adopted by the Eastern Mennonite Board of Missions and Charities, Jan. 23, 1985.

person is of value and has significant things to share. This does not mean you hide your deeply felt conviction that your salvation is through Messiah Jesus and that all people can come to God only through him. At the 1986 conference, Walter Riggans of All Nations Christian College in England, stated "Our humility should spring from personal conviction of our sinful lives and imperfect understanding, not lack of confidence in the power of the gospel nor in its universal need."

Dialogue is significant because it enables us to talk to one another as Jew and Gentile rather than to remain separated and isolated. As the dialogue progresses, there may be opportunities directed by the Holy Spirit to explain the gospel of Jesus. Even at the beginning of dialogue, Christian participants need to be clear about their commitment to Jesus as *the way* to be reconciled to God for *all* people.

Dialogue may include visiting a local synagogue to learn about the worship of Jewish neighbors. Several persons from our church visited a local synagogue on a Friday evening. The synagogue bulletin included a note of welcome to our group. Before the service began, the rabbi publicly explained the synagogue for our benefit. Afterward we shared in bar mitzvah refreshments with our hosts. Dialogue may include working together as Jews and Christians against community ills. It includes mutual respect. It does not need to exclude the right to confidently proclaim the gospel of Messiah Jesus.

Other areas of commonality

Christians and Jews share the First Covenant Scriptures, the Tenach. We worship the same God. One can witness from the Hebrew Scriptures without quickly jumping to the New Covenant Scriptures.

Both Jews and Christians are deeply committed to family. The family is an important component of experiencing faith and of passing faith on from generation to generation. Maintaining marriage and family faithfulness is a significant priority. Christians and Jews can mutually encourage each other in supporting the value of family.

For some Christians, suffering as a people is an experience shared with Jewish people. We have seen how Jewish people have suffered severely over the centuries. To be a Jew is to inherit a history of pain, misunderstanding by the larger world, persecution, and martyrdom, often at the hands of Christians. Groups of Christians like the Anabaptists (from whom have come Mennonites, Brethren in Christ, and other groups), also know a heritage of suffering. In fact, one reference from the Reformation era reported that Anabaptists were to be treated like Jews. Thousands of Anabaptists met their deaths by burning at the stake or by drowning, frequently after horrible torturing. Death came at the hands of other Christians of the state church who abhorred the Anabaptists' refusal to baptize infants[2] and their commitment generally to take the way of peacemaking rather than to take up the sword. Many Anabaptist Mennonites fled to the New World of America to find a place where they could practice their religious faith in peace and without disturbance.

Black American Christians can also identify with the experience of suffering, because of the history of slavery of blacks in colonial America and pre-Civil War United States. Of course, even after the Civil War and up to the present, the suffering of blacks and the denial of civil rights has continued. This suffering also came at the hands of Christians. The slave owners were the new Pharaoh, and Abraham Lincoln became a modern-day Moses to the slaves. The cry, "Let my people go!" from the book of Exodus echoed through the cotton fields and slave shanties of the South. Interestingly but not ironically, in the fight for

---

2 Anabaptists understand adult, believers' baptism to be the scriptural norm. ("Anabaptist"—rebaptizer—was the name given to this group because of rebaptizing persons who had been baptized as infants.)

civil rights for American blacks, Jews were in the forefront in crusading for fairness, equality, and justice. In the past, Jews and blacks have frequently worked together in resisting racial discrimination.

Justice for the oppressed and disadvantaged is a common concern of many Jews and of many Christians who believe the gospel touches the whole of life, social inequities as well as spiritual iniquities. For many, the area of working for justice in human relations is another point of commonality between Jews and Christians. It is the desire to tear down walls of racism and prejudice and to build bridges of constructive and positive relationships between peoples and races. Certainly Jesus was a model for love in interpersonal relationships.

Messiah called his followers to put away the sword and to love their enemies. He gave respect to women, children, Samaritans, and other social outcasts. He demonstrated that God loves the whole world and commissioned his followers to go into the whole world and make disciples of all nations.

A place to begin

Points of commonality between Jews and Christians are places to begin in relating to one another and respecting one another. We are not totally different from each other. We have many areas of common concern.

Yet there is one major difference and point of departure. That point is a person, the person of Messiah. Evangelical Christians believe Messiah has come and that he has commissioned them to proclaim to all people, including Jews, salvation through him, the Jewish Jesus of Galilee, God's Anointed Messenger. We dare not let dialogue deter us from that proclamation.

Study questions for reflection and discussion

1. Do you see the emphasis on points of commonality between Jews and Christians as helpful or as a hindrance in witnessing for Messiah to Jewish people?

2. How would you define "dialogue"? Do you see dangers in the process of dialogue between Christians and Jews? Do you see positive factors in dialogue?

3. Is dialogue biblical? Can you think of scriptural principles and examples for dialogue as a part of Christian witness? Consider Paul's experience in Athens described in Acts 17:16-33.

4. What are points of commonality where you personally can identify with Jewish friends and neighbors? Can these be starting points for a witness about Jesus?

11

Witnessing—with Confidence and Sensitivity

God's work

Ken Jacobs describes his coming to faith in Messiah as God following after him. But God used people to witness to Ken.

Ken remembers people who told him as a child about God's love. The message of their words stayed with him through the trauma of early junior high experiences: moving, adjustment to a new school, academic struggles, his parents' divorce, severe despair, final preparations for bar mitzvah, and a digestive disorder.

Neighbors shared the gospel with Ken, and he began to read the Scriptures. He believed Jesus was likely the Messiah, but he was struggling as a teenager, even dabbling into the occult. In senior high, new friends directed Ken to a prayer group, and there he met a Jewish man who said he was a believer in Messiah Jesus. This introduction shocked Ken. He thought he was the only Jewish person who believed Jesus was Messiah.

Ken continued to read the Scriptures and to discuss with his friends. He became convinced that what he was searching for could only be found in Jesus; he professed faith in Messiah and began attending a congregation made

up of Jewish and Gentile believers. Ken went on to gradu-
ate from Bible college.

God uses people to proclaim the good news of Messiah and salvation. He used people to touch Ken Jacobs. Step
by step the Spirit of God followed Ken and led him to
faith.

Will you be a witness for Messiah?

Our motivation

Let's review our motivation:

1. The Scriptures point to making witnessing to Jewish people a priority (Romans 1:16).

2. God promises to bless those who bless his chosen
   people (Genesis 12:1-3). A primary way to bless
   Jewish people is to share the gospel of Messiah
   with them.

3. In that same promise to Abraham in Genesis 12,
   God said he would bless all peoples on earth
   through Abraham. Bringing the gospel to Jewish
   people helps to fulfill God's missionary purposes in
   the world.

4. Salvation has come to us through the Jewish people
   and our Jewish Savior—Jesus (John 4:22). The best
   way to repay our debt to Jewish people is to share
   Jesus (Yeshua) with them.

5. In Romans 11:11-15, although Paul proclaimed that
   Israel's falling away from God brought great riches
   to the world through many Gentiles coming to
   know God as the gospel came to them, he went on
   to assert that even greater riches will result through
   the salvation (fullness) of Jewish people. It will be
   like life from the dead, he exults! In verses 26 and
   27 of that chapter, Paul indicates that a great many
   Jewish people will believe in Jesus before the end of
   time. It appears that God will again use the Jewish

people as a special witness to the world. Our witness can help enhance God's kingdom purposes.

6. Also in that Romans 11 passage, Paul encouraged Gentile believers to make Jewish people "jealous" for life in Messiah Jesus. Tragically, Gentile Christendom has often done the opposite—pushing Jewish people away from Messiah through persecution and killing! The call to Gentile believers is to live the kind of loving, joyful, and peaceful life in Messiah that will attract Jewish and other people, helping to make them desire that same kind of life.

A story in the Gospels helps to illustrate that last point. In Luke 7, an unnamed Gentile centurion had so impressed the Jewish community by his love for them and his actions on their behalf (building them a synagogue) that several Jewish elders went at the centurion's request and pleaded earnestly with Jesus to come and heal the man's dying servant. Jesus commended the great faith of the centurion.

In *The Olive Tree Connection*[1], John Fischer quotes a prominent Jewish lecturer: "The Jewish nature and soul needs to know God; it must be told about God. Our souls are looking for God and are trying to know God, and no one has told them." Fischer refers to a rabbi who said that in our society people want something more tangible in religion than the abstractness that Judaism has generally provided. The rabbi even admitted that the Jesus movement has all the answers. Jewish people deserve an opportunity to respond to the invitation of the gospel.

---

1 Downers Grove, Illinois: InterVarsity Press, 1983, p. 19.

A place to begin

Appreciating things we as Christian believers hold in common with the Jewish community is a place to begin. We must move beyond that starting point to the place of sharing Jesus.

Consider further beginning points. Take an interest in Jewish culture. Add bagels and cream cheese, matzo ball soup, or other foods to your menu on occasion. Be alert to articles in your newspaper related to Jewish concerns. Browse through a Jewish newspaper. Read author Chaim Potok's novels such as *The Chosen* and *The Promise* to understand Jewish life. See a production of *Fiddler on the Roof*. Visit a synagogue. Collect some Jewish artifacts for your home. Visit Israel if you can. To help understand the gigantic leap it is for a Jewish person to profess faith in Messiah Jesus, read Stan Telchin's *Betrayed!* Telchin tells his story of coming to faith as a result of his researching the New Testament, intending to disprove his daughter's newfound faith.

Learn to know Jewish friends as people. Do not ever allow yourself to view people as "objects" or "scalps" for conversion. Genuine love and concern can continue friendships even though people reject Messiah. The grace and wisdom of the Holy Spirit can guide us in bringing friendship and evangelism together.

Lifestyle witnessing

Is witnessing for Jesus a way of life, or is it something we only do at certain scheduled times? I can say that my whole life is a witness for Messiah and make no effort to verbalize my faith to others. On the other hand, I can assume that witnessing means handing out gospel literature, knocking on doors, making phone calls to strangers, carrying placards with gospel slogans and chanting a catchy jingle about the good news. Having done such witnessing ventures, I might neglect the spiritual need of my next-door neighbor or the person I work with.

The challenge is to simply develop friendships with Jewish acquaintances and to naturally live your life in Messiah before them. We are not emphasizing religion or Christianity but a relationship with God through Messiah. We point people to God and to Messiah as *the* way to God.

Be spontaneous and friendly in your relationships. Talk about your faith in a natural kind of way. Do not be defensive or argumentative.

Be careful about using set formulas to share the gospel. Instead, you might share about your personal relationship with God, talk about answers to prayer, and tell your friend you will pray for needs which may arise in his or her life and family.

You can ask leading questions about your friend's faith or religious practices, such as Jewish festivals, doing so with sensitivity. You may be able to share your faith in return.

Express love to your friend, but do not be "gushy" about it. Simply show it in natural ways. You might express your appreciation, as appropriate, to your friend for the fact that your salvation has come through the Jewish people, through the Jewish Messiah.

You could talk about the way God has preserved the Jewish people, despite terrible persecution, and how God is continuing to work out his purposes through his people. As your friend is open, you can share Scripture with him or her, preferably from a Jewish version of the Hebrew Scriptures.[2] When appropriate, you can discuss Messianic prophecies (see chapter thirteen), give your friend a copy of the Gospel of Matthew (especially written for a Jewish audience), or give him or her a copy of the prophecy edi-

---

2 Be aware that verse numbering and the order of books varies somewhat from your "Old Testament" version. (You can use the table of contents.)

tion of the New Testament. (These Testaments, which can
be purchased from the International Bible Society, emphasize in bold print the references to the Hebrew Scriptures.)
You may wish to invite your friend to a non-threatening
Bible study.

Avoid any anti-Semitic language. Do not join in negative criticism of Judaism or of rabbis. Do not even agree
with negative comments your friend may make about
Judaism; instead, be positive in your talk. Do not use trick-
ery or deception. Be "up front" about your faith and your
concern for your friend's relationship with God, but do not
be "pushy."

Be humble, knowing the history of Christian anti-
Semitism, and recognizing there is much you do not know
about Judaism. Yet, be confident as a witness, along with
sensitivity and caring. Time is important, time to be with
and to get to know your friends. A relationship carefully
nurtured can provide opportunities to witness about Messiah. Do not be in a rush. Give the Spirit time to work in
your friend's life. Sometimes the fruit of witnessing comes
years after the relationship began. Lifestyle witnessing is
not "hit and run." It is "love and relate."

Prayer is the key!

"No one comes to faith in God apart from prayer,"
someone has said. Witnessing needs to be bathed in prayer.
Fruitful witnessing is not human effort; it is done in the
power of the Holy Spirit. The gospel "is the power of God
for the salvation of everyone who believes: first for the Jew,
then for the Gentile" (Romans 1:16).

Prayer unleashes that power to effectively minister to
people. Through prayer, the Spirit softens people's hearts.
And he gives guidance and courage to us as witnesses.

Perhaps you do not have Jewish acquaintances. Pray
for God to bring you into contact with Jewish people.
Maybe you are fearful about witnessing. Pray for God to
give you courage. You may be aware of anti-Semitic atti-

tudes in your heart. Pray for God to cleanse your heart and to give you a heart of love. Ask him to prepare the hearts of friends to be open to the gospel.

You can pray with Christian friends in order to increase your prayer resources. The Shofar Committee, with which I work, has solicited the prayer help of a number of senior citizens in a Christian retirement community. These older believers delight in praying for a witness to Jewish people. What a marvelous spiritual resource!

Sharing answers to prayer is an excellent way to witness to friends. Talking only about having peace and joy in a relationship with God may be confusing, because other religious groups also give that testimony. Sharing how God has answered prayer can be a vital part of Christian witness.

An answer to prayer!

Moishe Rosen, founder and director of Jews for Jesus, says that it was the power of prayer that brought him to faith in Messiah. When someone began witnessing to him, Moishe was afraid what the man had to say might be true, and he wanted to hear no more. He insisted the man must stop witnessing to him.

This Christian gentleman submitted to Moishe's wishes. However, he prayed regularly for Moishe. His family joined him in prayer for Moishe's salvation, praying at every meal time for *four* years.

Moishe's wife, also Jewish, came to faith first. Then she, this faithfully praying family, and several other believers all prayed fervently for Moishe. In seven weeks, Moishe reports, the Holy Spirit had convicted him that the Bible is true and that Jesus is real. Except for prayer, Moishe writes, it might have been seven years instead of seven weeks. Or maybe never at all![3]

---

3 Told in *Share the New Life With a Jew*, by Moishe and Ceil Rosen (Chicago: Moody Press, 1976), p. 67.

Study questions for reflection and discussion

1. What is your personal motivation for witnessing to Jewish people?

2. What fears do you have about witnessing, and how might you overcome them?

3. How could you begin building witnessing friendships with Jewish people? Are there Jewish people living in your neighborhood? Be alert to Jewish coworkers, business people, your doctor, and others. If you have access to greeting cards for Jewish festival occasions, you might send them as gestures of friendship.

4. Who could be a prayer partner(s) with you, so that you could encourage one another in witnessing?

5. One can share the gospel message using only passages from the Hebrew Scriptures ("Old Testament"). Consider the following texts:

   a. All are sinners.—Isaiah 64:6, Ecclesiastes 7:20

   b. Sin separates from God.—Isaiah 59:1, 2

   c. Sin is taken away by blood atonement and by the sacrifice of Messiah.—Leviticus 17:11, Isaiah 53:3-8

   d. Salvation/righteousness comes by faith in God.—Genesis 15:6

   e. God freely offers pardon to the repentant sinner.—Isaiah 55:6, 7

   f. God calls those who seek his face into a community of the people of God.—Psalm 95:6, 7; Hosea 2:23

   g. God calls his people to act justly, love mercy, and walk humbly before him—to live out their faith.—Micah 6:8

12

Witnessing—Following Through

Demonstrating for Yeshua

"Down with death! Up with Yeshua! Down with death! Up with Yeshua!"

"Who're you gonna call? Deathbuster! Who're you gonna call? Yeshua!"

About eight of us were marching up and down South Street, chanting slogans like the ones above, and carrying placards that proclaimed catch-phrases like "Yeshua is the Deathbuster!" We all wore blue T-shirts stamped with the name Jesus front and back, shaped in the form of a star of David. A colleague followed us, handing out broadsides[1] and being alert to striking up conversations with people on the street. The Friday night crowd occasionally poked fun at us. One person argued that Jesus would have been more diplomatic.

Our outreach was particularly focused on reaching Jewish people, but we were certainly interested in Gentile contacts also. Why choose such a method? Weren't we looking a little stupid? This hardly looked like friendship evangelism.

---

1 Broadsides are pamphlets with cartoon drawings, a catchy title, and an evangelistic message hand-lettered and to the point.

We were making a point, a bit dramatically, being a little crazy for Yeshua. And hopefully the message would strike home for some people. As we dispersed to distribute broadsides, we hoped the preceding demonstration had served to arouse people's curiosity. It is one method of witnessing.

The street is neutral turf. People are anonymous. They may well be more receptive to taking literature on the street where no one knows them than they would be at home. Even though the literature is stuffed away somewhere, people have given testimonies stating how years later such literature was used by God to touch their hearts.

Such somewhat confrontational styles of witnessing will reach some people with the gospel. This is especially true when prayer has prepared the way, asking God to direct to people who are searching spiritually. Contacts, with names, addresses, and phone numbers, can be followed up later.

Some witnesses have participated in TV panel discussions (or debates!) with rabbis or other Jewish leaders, taking the gospel public in a dramatic kind of way. Love for a lively discussion will make such an encounter productive in reaching some people.

Going public in such dramatic ways with witnessing helps to reinforce for us believers that we are indeed called to be witnesses for Messiah. It may prod us to be more faithful in lifestyle witnessing and friendship evangelism relationships.

Watching our words

Whether in relationship evangelism or in more dramatic interaction, it is important to be aware of terminology which can be offensive to Jewish people. Avoid the term "conversion." It brings to mind "forced conversions" to the Christian faith in past eras when a Jewish person may have had to choose between death or "converting" to Christianity. In addition, the Jewish person may think you are expecting him to convert from being Jewish to accepting Christianity. The truth is that a person remains Jewish even when he professes faith in Messiah, even though many Jewish people may not be able to accept that. We are calling people to turn from sinfulness to faith in God through Messiah the Savior, not to turn from Jewishness to Christianity. "Turn!" is a very Jewish term, for the Hebrew prophets were constantly calling Israel to turn, or return, to their God.

Do not use the term, "You Jews." It is better to say, "Jewish people," "Jewish man," or "Jewish woman." The term "Jewess" for Jewish girl or woman can sometimes be seen as derogatory, and it is better not to use it. Be aware that with one another, Jewish people may use terms that would be unwise for non-Jewish people to use. You may even hear Jewish people use anti-Semitic terms in conversation, but Gentiles (especially believers) should never be caught saying them. (See the beginning of chapter seven.)

In talking about the Jewish Scriptures, avoid saying "Old Testament." It makes it sound out of date or antiquated. It is better to say "the Tenach" (acronym in Hebrew for the Law, the Prophets, and the Writings) or "the Hebrew Scriptures."

The term "Jesus Christ" (especially "Christ") associated with the cry, "Christ killer!" tends to be offensive. You might say "Yeshua Hamashiach"—"Jesus the Messiah" in Hebrew—or "Messiah Jesus." However, do not hide that it is Jesus the Messiah you are talking about. Moishe Rosen tells the story (in the book referred to in the last chapter) of the Jewish woman who came to services and professed how she loved "Yeshua." But when she discovered to her horror that "Yeshua" was the same as "Jesus," she left in a huff and never returned to those services again.

A general rule is to not act overly "mushy" in professing love for Jewish people, nor on the other hand, to use demeaning language or tell stories or jokes critical of Jewish people. Again, relate naturally as a friend.

Beware of Christian symbols or practices that can be offensive. Wearing a cross will not endear you to Jewish people, because of the stigma of that symbol being connected with the Crusades and the Inquisition. Exhibiting pictures of Jesus may seem like idolatry to some Jewish people.[2] If you are a guest in a Jewish home, and wine is served at the meal, and that is a problem for you, it is better to merely touch it to your lips than to make a little speech about not drinking alcoholic beverages. Accepting Jewish dance, even as a part of Messianic Jewish worship services, may be an area where God wants to stretch you to be flexible.

Be careful about categorizing!

It is helpful to be aware of the various Jewish denominations, such as Orthodox, Conservative, and Reform, but avoid putting Jewish people in boxes. Again, relate person to person. Ask leading questions to draw the person out, without getting too personal. Share from your own life experiences.

Some Jewish people are basically secular or pagan, without any religious affiliation. You may wish to simply relate Jesus in your witness, or you might raise their curiosity by expressing your interest in Jewish faith and culture.

Do not assume that all Jewish people have a vast knowledge of the Tenach. Many do not, even some who are religious. One young Jewish believer said that her Christian friends assumed she knew all about the Hebrew Scriptures and were a little afraid to talk with her about them. But she said, in fact, she knew little, and as a new

2 One cannot avoid being completely unoffensive. There will always be the offense of the gospel. 1 Corinthians 1:23 states that the preaching of the cross is a stumbling block to Jews and foolishness to Gentiles. We do not need to be unnecessarily offensive. Having said that, I know that wearing a T-shirt with "Jesus" in the shape of a star of David can certainly be offensive. It is also an attention-arouser, helping to make people stop and think.

believer in Messiah, she was only then delving into the Hebrew Scriptures.

Objections will come!

It is helpful to be aware of some objections which Jewish people might raise with you as you relate to them. Perhaps foremost is, "You can't believe in Jesus and still be Jewish." I already alluded to this objection. One may be Buddhist or pagan and still be accepted as Jewish, but generally to believe in Jesus is to ostracize oneself from the Jewish community. A Jewish person often simply assumes that he or she does not even consider Jesus. Or, if one does indeed consider the claims of Messiah, there may be great fear of rejection from one's family and Jewish community. You can assure your friend that he or she would still be Jewish after believing in Jesus, that Jesus was Jewish, that his disciples and the earliest believers in Jesus were Jewish, and that all (except perhaps Luke) of the New Testament writers were Jewish. To believe in Jesus is a very Jewish thing to do. If your Jewish friend is considering faith in Messiah, or sincerely inquiring, introduce him or her to a Messianic Jewish believer if you are a Gentile believer. Frequently Jewish believers, or inquirers, have felt very much alone, feeling that no other Jewish person thinks about Jesus as they do. It is a relief and encouragement for them to learn to know Messianic Jewish believers. Assure your friend that one is Jewish by birth, and that believing in Jesus does not change that. In fact, many times a Jewish person embraces his or her Jewishness even more fully after believing in Messiah Jesus.

The second big objection, related to the first, is that historically Christians have persecuted and killed many Jewish people, as we have seen, and it is therefore extremely difficult for Jews to believe in Jesus who is identified with Gentile Christians who have killed Jews and slandered Jewish people as "Christ killers!" In our witnessing, we need to: abhor this past history of hatred, express sorrow to Jewish people for the sins of the past against them, relate in love to Jewish people, repudiate all anti-Semitism, and share our witness with a humble and repentant attitude, yet with loving confidence. Once when I was handing out literature on the street, a Jewish woman threw at me a response something like this, "How can I dare believe in your message after all that Christians have done to the Jewish people?" We cannot respond defensively. Rather we respond with humble sorrow. Yet we cannot let that deter us from presenting the Messiah to his own Jewish people.

Jewish people may also claim that Jesus could *not* have been the Messiah, for various reasons. Messiah was not to have suffered, it is suggested by many. One might share Isaiah 53, pointing out that the suffering servant is an individual person and thus could not be only the nation of Israel, which is often the interpretation given. One can also comment to your Jewish friend that Jewish sages of the past have seen Isaiah 53 as referring to the Messiah. Some saw two Messiahs, one who would come as a suffering savior if Israel was sinning and one who would come as a victorious conqueror if Israel was living faithfully. Of course, we understand that Messiah Jesus realized the first role in his first advent and that he will come as conquering king in his second appearance.

Another objection is that Jesus could not have been the Messiah because he did not bring world peace. A rabbi whom I once talked with told me just that. There is also a story of a rabbi in Europe who was asked whether Messiah had come. He went to the window, looked out, and said, no, Messiah had not come, because things continued the same as before. You can share with your Jewish friend our understanding that Messiah will come a second time to bring peace. We affirm that Jesus does bring us inner peace and that he calls us to be peacemakers as the children of God. Also, recall that Messiah said he did not come to bring peace but a sword. Families will be split as individuals in a family give allegiance to Jesus. There is a cross to bear in following Messiah. Unfortunately, much of the reason there has not often been peace is because of warring Christians.

Your Jewish friend may say that Jesus was just a good teacher, that he did not claim to be Messiah. However, he did make that claim in John 4:26. Also, in verses 30 and 36 of John 10, Jesus claimed oneness with Father God and that he was the Son of God. In Matthew 9:1-8, Jesus forgave sins, something only God can truly do. Jesus also healed by the power of God. Jesus did indeed exhibit the signs of Messiahship.

A Jewish acquaintance may object to you that Christians believe in three gods. Affirm that we do believe in one God, but that God's oneness is a composite oneness, just as husband and wife become "one flesh." The Hebrew Scriptures affirm God's oneness in the great Shema, "Hear, O Israel, the Lord our God, the Lord is one!" The same root word is used in Hebrew to speak of the oneness of God in the Shema and the oneness of husband and wife in Genesis 2. Again, it is a composite oneness. The Hebrew Scriptures also speak of the Spirit expression of God and the Son expression of God. (See Genesis 1:2, Psalm 2:7 and Proverbs 30:4.)

Jewish people may believe that since there is no longer any Temple, people can be acceptable to God by prayers and good deeds. The concept of our being sinners may be rejected by your Jewish friend. You can remind him or her that the Hebrew prophets again and again declared to the people their sinfulness and unfaithfulness and that Leviticus asserts that blood must be shed as a sacrifice for sin. Messiah came to be that sacrifice once for all as the perfect Lamb of God. We need to accept his saving work for us by faith in him.

A faith decision, follow-through, and fellowship

When you sense a Jewish friend is at the point of deciding to place faith in Messiah Jesus, you can carefully explain that this is a total commitment. Emphasize that it is decisively turning from sin to God in repentance and going a new direction by the power of God's Spirit. The Spirit of God will transform him or her into a new creation in Messiah Jesus. This is a lifelong process. Lead your friend through a prayer of repentance before God, commitment of his or her life to Messiah as Lord, and openness to the Holy Spirit's filling. Introduce your friend to other Messianic believers. Encourage your friend to share with some other people about his or her newfound faith in Messiah. Instruct them in regular reading of the Scriptures and in prayer. Guide them in beginning to submit every area of life to Messiah as Master and Lord. Prepare them for spiritual warfare and to stand strong against the evil one's attacks.

Direct your friend in finding fellowship within the body of believers in Messiah. Help him or her consider the options of a Messianic congregation, if one is nearby, or a church that will allow a Jewish believer to be a part of the body without needing to lay aside his or her Jewishness. In fact, you may be able to find a church that encourages some expression of the Jewish roots of the Christian faith. There may also be the option of an informal Messianic fellowship to embrace the Jewishness of your friend's new faith while also participating in full-fledged church membership.

Stand with your friend in any possible rejection from family which he or she may face because of commitment to Messiah Jesus. The new Messianic believer may need to lean heavily on other believers for support in the early days of his or her new life in Messiah. Encourage your friend to be the best son or daughter or sister or brother he or she can be within the family. One Messianic believer decided to do just that, and as I recall the story, he saw his rabbi father also come to faith in Messiah.

> For I am not ashamed of the Gospel, because it is the power of God for the salvation of everyone who

believes, first for the Jew, then for the Gentile. (Romans 1:16)

Study questions for reflection and discussion

1. Role play a discussion with a Jewish friend involving some of the objections mentioned in this chapter.

2. How do you respond to witnessing which is somewhat confrontational, such as that described in the beginning of this chapter?

3. In your own words, how would you explain to a Jewish friend the way to salvation at the point of decision?

4. What are the next few steps of obedience to Messiah for you in being a witness to Jewish people?

5. Another helpful book on witness to Jewish people is Barry Rubin's *You Bring the Bagels—I'll Bring the Gospel* published by Chosen Books.

13

Jesus the Messiah

Encountered by Messiah

Abe Sandler, Jewish teenager, sat in a Bible study led by George Gruen in Philadelphia. George was a friend to young Jewish fellows, played basketball with them, and gathered them for Bible studies. On one particular day, George read to the fellows from Isaiah 53. Abe heard, "But he was pierced for our transgressions, he was crushed for our iniquities; the punishment that brought us peace was upon him, and by his wounds we are healed. . . ."

When he finished reading, George asked, "Who do you think this is talking about?" Shot back young Abe, "Jesus—but I don't believe the New Testament!" George handed the Bible to Abe so that he could see where George had read from. To his amazement, Abe saw that the passage was not from the New Testament but from the Hebrew Scriptures.

Abe thought George might have tricked them, so he checked it out in his own Jewish Bible. Sure enough, it was there. The passage was a key to Abe's subsequently believing in Jesus as Messiah. When he confessed his belief to his parents, they took him to see the rabbi. The rabbi counseled him to have nothing to do with such belief, despite the Isaiah 53 passage. Abe, however, convinced that this Scripture in the Jewish Bible was for Jewish people, and that it did speak about Messiah Jesus, ignored the rabbi's advice.

Today Abe Sandler is active in witnessing to Jewish people and in calling others to do the same. The prophecy of Isaiah 53 was used by the Holy Spirit to turn him to personal faith in Messiah Jesus.

* * * * * * * * * * *

Two distraught figures plodded along the road, their eyes downcast, their hearts heavy. Their hopes had been dashed by events of recent days. A third person began to walk alongside of them and asked what it was they were talking about. They told him, "We had hoped Jesus of Nazareth would be Israel's redeemer, but he has been crucified. There are reports of a vision of angels who said Jesus was alive again, but. . . ." Then the stranger responded to their doubt and confusion.

> He said to them, "How foolish you are, and how slow of heart to believe all that the prophets have spoken! Did not the Christ have to suffer these things and then enter his glory?" And beginning with Moses and all the Prophets, he explained to them what was said in all the Scriptures concerning himself. (Luke 24:25-27)

Wouldn't you like to have that conversation of Jesus with the two people on the way to Emmaus on a videocassette, to be able to hear directly from the Lord himself how the Hebrew Scriptures prophesy of him?

Sometimes we have been turned off by prophecy speakers or writers who seem to go overboard in explaining how "that prophecy" of Scripture means "this event" today or in the near future. We may become especially upset with those who set dates for the Lord's return. Nevertheless, we cannot simply cast prophecy aside because we think some Bible teachers, although well-meaning, have exploited it.

Obviously Jesus used prophecy in his teaching. Used in a right manner, with discernment and direction of the Spirit, a study of biblical prophecy and fulfillment affirms and enhances faith and our understanding of the Scriptures. Such a study can show the trustworthiness of God and the reliability of the Scriptures. Bible prophecy is a helpful means for witnessing about Messiah to Jewish people. Let's take a look then at Messianic prophecy.

First promise of a Savior

God wasted no time. Immediately after the Fall, God promised to Adam and Eve a Savior who would one day come and crush the power of the evil one who had deceived them. Actually the promise was spoken to the serpent himself.

> "And I will put enmity between you and the woman, and between your offspring and hers; he will crush your head and you will strike his heal." (Genesis 3:15)

The devil would one day in the crucifixion of Jesus "strike the heal" of Messiah born of a woman. However, in that death and his subsequent resurrection, Messiah Jesus would deal Satan a mortal blow to his head and rescue those who turn to him from Satan's domination.

> But when the time had fully come, God sent his Son, born of a woman, born under law. . . . (Galatians 4:4)

> Since the children have flesh and blood, he too shared in their humanity so that by his death he might destroy him who holds the power of death—that is, the devil—and free those who all their lives were held in slavery by their fear of death. (Hebrews 2:14-15)

The promise of blessing through Abraham

Compare the promise given to Abraham in Genesis with the fulfillment presented by the Apostle Paul in Galatians.

> ". . . And through your offspring [literally, seed] all nations on earth will be blessed, because you have obeyed me." (Genesis 22:18)

He redeemed us in order that the blessing given to
Abraham might come to the Gentiles through Christ
Jesus, so that by faith we might receive the promise of
the Spirit. (Galatians 3:14)

The promises were spoken to Abraham and to his
seed. The Scripture does not say "and to seeds,"
meaning many people, but "and to your seed," meaning one person, who is Christ. (Galatians 3:16)

If you belong to Christ, then you are Abraham's seed,
and heirs according to the promise. (Galatians 3:29)

Messiah was to come through the Jewish people, the
descendants of the Patriarch Abraham.

The promise of a ruler through Judah

Judah was one of Abraham's great-grandsons, one of
the twelve sons of Jacob. David belonged to the tribe of
Judah. And Jesus would be born to the same family line.
As he was dying, Jacob prophesied concerning his sons.
Note part of the prophecy given about his son Judah:

The scepter will not depart from Judah, nor the ruler's
staff from between his feet, until he comes to whom it
belongs and the obedience of the nations is his. (Genesis 49:10)

An alternate translation for "until he comes" is "until
Shiloh comes." Shiloh was seen as a Messianic name. Regardless, the verse speaks of one to come to whom the
ruler's staff belongs. Can that be other than Messiah Jesus?

In his book, *Evidence That Demands a Verdict*, Josh
McDowell explains that the Jewish legal council, the Sanhedrin, held the power of capital punishment (thus hold-
ing "the scepter" so to speak) until a few years after Jesus'
birth, when the Romans took this power from them.
McDowell quotes an ancient Jewish source, in which the
Sanhedrin is crying out, "Woe unto us, for the scepter has
departed from Judah, and the Messiah has not come."[1] The
Messiah had come, but they were unaware of him.

---

1 From Josh McDowell's *Evidence That Demands A Verdict* (1979), pp. 168-
170. (For bibliographic information, see footnote 3, this chapter.)

The promise of a prophet like Moses

In Deuteronomy 18:15-19, Moses told the Jewish nation that God did not wish for them to look to occult sources for direction, and in that context he spoke of another prophet like himself that God would raise up to speak the word of the Lord.

In a sermon recorded in Acts 3, Peter was proclaiming the Messiah and announced that Messiah fulfilled the Deuteronomy prophecy of Moses:

> "For Moses said, 'The Lord your God will raise up for you a prophet like me from among your own people; you must listen to everything he tells you. Anyone who does not listen to him will be completely cut off from among his people.'" (Acts 3:22-23)

The greater Prophet had come!

The greater Son of David

God established a covenant with King David that his descendants would rule forever. (See 2 Samuel 7:16 and Psalm 89:3-4.) Literally, in terms of human kings, that has not occurred. But the Messianic King, born of the family of David, has fulfilled that covenant promise. (See Matthew 1:1.) In discussing this one day with the teachers of the law, Jesus pointed out (to the consternation of the teachers!) that Messiah is not only the son of David but also David's "Lord"! Messiah is more than human—he is the divine Lord! (See Matthew 22:41-46, referring to Psalm 110:1.)

Born of a virgin

How familiar these words are:

> Therefore the Lord himself will give you a sign: The virgin will be with child and will give birth to a son, and will call him Immanuel. (Isaiah 7:14)

This was spoken by Isaiah the prophet to the stubborn King Ahaz who did not wish to ask God for a sign that the Lord would indeed rescue Ahaz's nation of Judah (the southern kingdom of Israel). Judah was facing military threats from the kings of Aram and Israel (the northern

Jewish kingdom). But God gave King Ahaz a sign and a promise anyway—the prophecy of a special birth.

The Hebrew word used, *almah*, can be translated either "young woman" or "virgin." There seems to be a two-fold fulfillment of Isaiah 7:14. In Ahaz's day a young woman (possibly even Isaiah's wife—see Isaiah 8:3-4) gave birth to a son who would not yet be grown by the time these two kings threatening Judah would be defeated by the king of Assyria. But there was also to be a further and greater fulfillment of this prophecy. The Septuagint Greek translation of the Hebrew Scriptures, a work done by Jewish scholars, used "virgin" in Isaiah 7:14. It would be to a virgin, Mary of Nazareth, that the true Immanuel ("God with us") would be born. The Gospel of Matthew announced this fulfillment. (See Matthew 1:22-23.)

The "Wonderful Counselor"

To whom else but Messiah Jesus could Isaiah be referring when he prophesied:

> For to us a child is born, to us a son is given, and the government will be on his shoulders. And he will be called Wonderful Counselor, Mighty God, Everlasting Father, Prince of Peace. Of the increase of his government and peace there will be no end. He will reign on David's throne and over his kingdom, establishing and upholding it with justice and righteousness from that time on and forever. The zeal of the LORD Almighty will accomplish this. (Isaiah 9:6-7)

This Scripture also proclaimed the divinity of Messiah. He is Mighty God and Everlasting Father. There will be no end to the increase of his government and peace. He will reign with justice forever.

The suffering servant

A suffering Messiah? Messiah was to be a conqueror, a deliverer! The nation of Israel would suffer—but not Messiah! Many Jewish people who look at Isaiah 53 would understand this passage to speak of the suffering of the

Jewish people. However, when Louis Goldberg was discussing with a rabbi that the offering of Isaiah 53:10 would need to be a perfect offering according to Leviticus 5, and that Israel could not be that, the rabbi replied, "Let's not discuss this any further."[2]

There have been some traditional Jewish interpretations that Isaiah 53 is a Messianic Scripture. But by the Middle Ages, in reaction to the Christian understanding of this passage, Jewish leaders in general argued that the suffering servant referred to the nation of Israel. As one carefully reads the passage, however, it clearly refers to an individual, not a nation. In addition, there is the difficulty of explaining how Israel could be pierced and crushed for their own (Israel's) transgressions and how the Lord could lay on Israel the iniquity of all of Israel (vv. 5, 6). At any rate, the Scripture is talking of one who takes upon himself the sins of another.

Recorded in Acts 8 is the story of Philip being led by the Spirit of God to witness to an Ethiopian man. The man from Ethiopia was reading from Isaiah 53, and when Philip joined him in his chariot, he asked Philip, "Tell me, please, who is the prophet talking about, himself, or someone else?" And the Bible reports that Philip began with that Isaiah 53 Scripture and told the Ethiopian treasury official the good news about Jesus.

"O Little Town of Bethlehem"

King Herod, disturbed by the advent of visitors from the East who were looking for a newborn king of the Jews, hurriedly called together the Jewish chief priests and teachers of the Law. He was threatened by the possible birth of a new king and asked where such a one was to be born. In Bethlehem, they replied, quoting from Micah 5:2:

---

2 From Louis Goldberg's *Our Jewish Friends*, (Neptune, NJ: Loizeaux Brothers, 1977), p. 126.

"But you, Bethlehem Ephrathah, though you are
small among the clans of Judah, out of you will come
for me one who will be ruler over Israel, whose origins are from of old, from ancient times."

An alternative translation is that this ruler's origins
are from days of eternity. Again, there is the testimony that
this is no ordinary ruler.

His specific place of birth was Bethlehem, David's
city. Messiah was born there, because a Roman emperor
decreed a taxation, and all had to register in their own
town. Joseph, married to Mary who had conceived Messiah by the Holy Spirit, went to Bethlehem, because he was a
descendant of David. There Mary gave birth to Jesus—
Messiah! How amazing and intricate are the acts of God!

The time of Messiah's birth

In addition to the Genesis 49:10 Scripture we looked
at, there is a most significant text in Daniel 9 about the time
of Messiah's arrival. Daniel cried out to God to remind
God that the seventy years of Jewish captivity in Babylon
were soon to be completed. Daniel apparently expected the
Messianic kingdom to appear at the end of the seventy
years.

God sent the angel Gabriel to Daniel with a special
message. Gabriel announced there would be seventy "sevens" until the time of Messiah would come in fullness—
490 years (70 X 7). At the end of sixty-nine sevens (483
years), Daniel is told, the Anointed One (Messiah) would
appear. Sometime after that, he would be "cut off" (killed).
The 483 years are to start with the issuing of a decree to
rebuild Jerusalem, and after the end of the 483 years, subsequent to Messiah's death, Jerusalem and the temple were
to be destroyed again.

There are several dates that might be considered for
the issuing of the decree to rebuild. One very possible date
suggested, that seems to fit well into the evidence, is 444
B.C.E. That is the year Artaxerxes gave to Nehemiah a

decree to rebuild the walls of Jerusalem. (See Nehemiah 2:1-8.) Using the Jewish prophetic year of 360 days brings the 483 years up to 33 C.E., about the year of Jesus' death. The temple and Jerusalem were overrun by the Roman Titus in 70 C.E. According to Daniel's prophecy then, Messiah would need to have appeared and died before 70 C.E.[3] This prophecy in Daniel 9 has helped in convincing a number of Jewish people that Jesus is Messiah (the "Anointed One"), leading them to become Messianic believers. Some Bible students believe the "seventieth seven" refers to prophecy yet to occur.

Types and figures of Messiah

In his book, *Evidence That Demands a Verdict*, Josh McDowell says there are several hundred references to Messiah in the Hebrew Scriptures. We have looked at a number of Messianic prophecies.

There are other ways in which the Hebrew Scriptures point to Messiah. First Covenant sacrifices are a type of the supreme sacrifice Messiah made when he laid down his life on the cross. His sacrifice fulfilled all other animal sacrifices once and for all. The slain Passover lamb, its blood splashed on the doorposts and lintel, was a type of the perfect Lamb of God. Messiah's death provides atonement for sin which fulfills the solemn Day of Atonement.

Messiah is the supreme, everlasting High Priest. He lives forever to be the Mediator between people and God.

There are other persons in the Hebrew Scriptures who are figures of Messiah. As death came to all people through the sin of the "first Adam," so in the "second Adam" (Messiah), life is available for all who believe in him. Joseph—sold for twenty pieces of silver by his brothers, established as a "savior" in Egypt (for both Gentiles

---

3 In *Evidence That Demands A Verdict*, Josh McDowell lays out in great detail the evidence he has gathered for this conclusion (San Bernardino, CA: Here's Life Publishers, Campus Crusade for Christ, Inc., 1979), pp. 170-175.

and Jews), and full of a forgiving spirit for his brothers—prefigures Messiah. Messiah was betrayed by one of his disciples for thirty pieces of silver, is Savior for all who trust him, and is the supreme model and agent of forgiveness.

Moses is a figure of the greater prophet and deliverer who came in Messiah. Joshua, whose name means "savior," prefigures Jesus, whose name also means "savior," ("You are to give him the name Jesus, because he will save his people from their sins," the angel told Joseph in Matthew 1:21).

Messiah has the heart of the prophet Jeremiah, who wept for his wayward people. He said, "I AM the Good Shepherd," which reminds us of Psalm 23 that states, "The Lord is my shepherd."

The I AMs of Messiah also take us back to God's statement to Moses at the burning bush, when he said, "Tell the people that I AM sent you." God identified himself as "I AM WHO I AM." Messiah, being God, is also "I AM."

These types and figures of Messiah could be used to point Jewish people to Messiah Jesus as prefigured already in the Hebrew Scriptures, the Jewish Bible.

Messiah incarnate in the Hebrew Scriptures?

God came to earth in human form in Messiah Jesus to be Savior! The incarnation (God appearing in human flesh) is a great wonder and an amazing miracle.

Suggesting that God also appeared in human form in stories of the Hebrew Scriptures may help Jewish people take the leap of faith to accept Jesus as God's incarnate Messiah.

Did God appear incarnate before the time of Messiah? I believe so. Consider the three men who visited Abraham to announce that he and Sarah would have a son. At the close of that visit, the Scriptures say Abraham walked with the men toward Sodom, and the Lord talked with Abra-

ham about the coming destruction of Sodom and Gomor-
rah. (See Genesis 18, especially v. 22.)

A few chapters later, in Genesis 32, as Jacob prepared
to meet his estranged brother Esau, he wrestled one night
with a man who appeared to him. The man gave Jacob a
new name, Israel, ". . . because you have struggled with
God and with men and have overcome." As Jacob left that
place, he testified, "I saw God face to face. . . ."

In Daniel 3, we read that King Nebuchadnezzar con-
demned three Jewish men to die in a fiery furnace, because
they would not bow to worship the huge image he had
erected. They were thrown bound into the fire, but the
king saw them walking around in the fire with a fourth
person whom he said, "looks like a son of the gods."
Awed, he ordered the men out of the fire, saw that they
were unharmed, and gave praise to the Most High God.

I suggest that any or all of these may have been pre-
incarnate appearances of Messiah. At the least, they are
divine appearance in human form which can be bridges of
preparation for helping Jewish people to accept Messiah as
God's "anointed Messenger." The Spirit of God can lift the
veil of unbelief to enable people to see that God has appeared in human form in Jesus of Nazareth. Having
looked at Messiah in the Hebrew Scriptures, we can understand Jesus' statement to the Jews that the Scriptures testi-
fy of him (John 5:39). Yet many failed to recognize him as
the Bringer of Life. What about us? What is our response to
the Messiah of the Scriptures?

Messiah, the center of Scripture

The Hebrew Scriptures tell the story of God meeting
his people and calling forth a people, in preparation for the
coming of his Son, the Messiah. The Tenach points toward
the coming of Messiah. When he came, Messiah filled full
with meaning the Tenach.

The Gospels present Messiah Jesus as God's supreme revelation of himself and his purposes. Jesus is the center point and central person of the biblical story.

The life and message of the early church centered on the death and resurrection of Jesus and his presence in their midst by the Holy Spirit. Paul's letters to the churches exalted Messiah and called the emerging clusters of believers to center their faith and fellowship on Messiah.

Prophecy about events yet to come center on Messiah also. The hope of God's people, now and for the future, in the present world and for eternity, focuses on Messiah Jesus. He is coming again, as Lord and King. He will gather his own to himself, and he will reign with the Father for ever and ever!

Prophecy yet to be fulfilled

Looking at prophecy that has been fulfilled is kind of like "Monday morning quarterbacking." How shall we handle prophecy yet to be fulfilled? Anyone who has delved only a little into the study of biblical prophecy is aware of the great variety of interpretations and viewpoints. One is tempted to simply ignore all study of prophecy, therefore. However, prophecy is a significant part of Scripture. We are told in the third verse of the prophetic book of Revelation,

> Blessed is the one who reads the words of this prophecy, and blessed are those who hear it and take to heart what is written in it, because the time is near. (Revelation 1:3)

Allow me to suggest some affirmations concerning prophecies of the future:

1. Messiah Jesus will bodily appear again and will reign forever as the Lord of lords.

> On that day his feet will stand on the Mount of Olives, east of Jerusalem. . . . (Zechariah 14:4a)

> The LORD will be king over the whole earth. On that day there will be one LORD, and his name the only name. (Zechariah 14:9)

"Men of Galilee," they [the angels] said, "why do you
stand here looking into the sky? This same Jesus, who
has been taken from you into heaven, will come back
in the same way you have seen him go into heaven."
(Acts 1:11)

Of the increase of his government and peace there
will be no end. He will reign on David's throne and
over his kingdom, establishing and upholding it with
justice and righteousness from that time on and forever. The zeal of the Lord Almighty will accomplish
this. (Isaiah 9:7)

These verses need not necessarily be seen in a strictly
millenial perspective. However we interpret the milleni-
um, we can affirm that Jesus will return to reign forever as
King of kings in his Father's everlasting kingdom.

2. Believers in Messiah Jesus should live now in
preparation for and in light of the return of Messiah.

Dear friends, now we are children of God, and what
we will be has not yet been made known. But we
know that when he appears, we shall be like him, for
we shall see him as he is. Everyone who has this hope
in him purifies himself, just as he is pure. (1 John 3:2-
3)

3. God still has a purpose to fulfill in the people of
Israel, the Jews.

I ask then: Did God reject his people? By no means! I
am an Israelite myself, a descendant of Abraham,
from the tribe of Benjamin. God did not reject his people, whom he foreknew. (Romans 11:1-2a)

Again I ask: Did they stumble so as to fall beyond re-
covery? Not at all! Rather, because of their transgression, salvation has come to the Gentiles to make Israel
envious. But if their transgression means riches for
the world, and their loss means riches for the Gentiles, how much greater riches will their fullness
bring! (Romans 11:11-12)

I do not want you to be ignorant of this mystery,
brothers, so that you may not be conceited: Israel has
experienced a hardening in part until the full number
of the Gentiles has come in. And so all Israel will be
saved. . . . (Romans 11:25-26a)

4. The powers of evil will be destroyed at the end time.

> And the devil, who deceived them, was thrown into the lake of burning sulfur, where the beast and the false prophet had been thrown. They will be tormented day and night for ever and ever. (Revelation 20:10)

5. All people will be judged in the end of time by God and sent either to eternal life or eternal death.

> "Multitudes who sleep in the dust of the earth will awake: some to everlasting life, others to shame and everlasting contempt." (Daniel 12:2)

> "Then he will say to those on his left, 'Depart from me, you who are cursed, into the eternal fire prepared for the devil and his angels.'. . . Then they will go away to eternal punishment, but the righteous to eternal life." (Matthew 25:41, 46. See also Revelation 21:6-8.)

6. To have eternal life will be to experience fully and wonderfully the presence of God.

> And I heard a loud voice from the throne saying, "Now the dwelling of God is with men, and he will live with them. They will be his people, and God himself will be with them and be their God. He will wipe every tear from their eyes. There will be no more death or mourning or crying or pain, for the old order of things has passed away." (Revelation 21:3-4)

7. In view of events yet to come, believers in Messiah are to faithfully proclaim to all people, to the Jew first and also to the Gentile, the good news of salvation through Messiah Jesus.

> "And this gospel of the kingdom will be preached in the whole world as a testimony to all nations, and then the end will come." (Matthew 24:14)

> I am talking to you Gentiles. Inasmuch as I am the apostle to the Gentiles, I make much of my ministry in the hope that I may somehow arouse my own people to envy and save some of them. (Romans 11:13-14)

Prophecy is important!

Is prophecy, biblical prophecy, important? The answer is "Yes!" In his book, *Bible Prophecy*, Paul Erb reported that one-third of the Bible is prophecy. He emphasized that biblical prophecy focuses upon and centers on Messiah Jesus. The book argues that a good understanding of biblical prophecy gives us proper perspective as believers in our time, knowing that history is not purposeless. God is working out his purposes, in history and in Messiah Jesus.

Much of this chapter focused on fulfilled Messianic prophecy. This can be especially significant for Jewish people in thinking through whether Jesus of Nazareth was indeed the anticipated Messiah. Part of the difficulty that needs to be worked through is the misunderstanding of the roles of Messiah—that he would appear both as suffering Savior (the first time) and also as triumphant king (the second time—yet to come). Jewish people have often anticipated Messiah's coming only in a triumphant role.

Details of prophecy concerning Messiah's first appearing were important, as we have seen. Therefore, we cannot simply dismiss as insignificant the details concerning prophecies of his second appearing. However, seeing that we stand in the "meanwhile" before his second appearing, rather than in the "after the fact" of his first appearing, let us be humble in our interpretations and viewpoints.

Messiah is coming back!

What we can affirm with confidence in all of this discussion of prophecy is the commission of Messiah Jesus to witness for him and to make disciples for him from all nations of people. For Jewish people or for anybody, true salvation will not come about by politics or by any human striving, but by the mercy and grace of Messiah. We are called to believe in and to witness for Messiah! For Messiah will appear again, and his return may be soon!

> "I, Jesus, have sent my angel to give you this testimony for the churches. I am the Root and the Offspring of David, and the bright Morning Star." The Spirit and the bride say, "Come!" And let him who hears

say, "Come!" Whoever is thirsty, let him come; and whoever wishes, let him take the free gift of the water of life. . . . He who testifies to these things says, "Yes, I am coming soon." Amen. Come, Lord Jesus. The grace of the Lord Jesus be with God's people. Amen. (Revelation 22:16, 17, 20, 21)

Study questions for reflection and discussion

1. What is the purpose of biblical prophecy?

2. Take one of the Messianic prophecies mentioned in this chapter and put it in your own words in a way that you might share it with a Jewish friend.

3. For you, what is the key theme or concern of biblical prophecy yet to be fulfilled?

4. How are biblical prophecy, hope, and our faithful following of Messiah Jesus all interrelated?

5. Summarize the whole biblical story (from Genesis to Revelation) in one paragraph, with Jesus as the central focus.

6. If you believe that Messiah Jesus is coming back (and maybe soon!), what changes will you make in how you live and witness?

7. Resources for some further reading and study on prophecy and the end times include: *Biblical Prophecy* by Paul Erb (Scottdale: Herald Press, 1978), and *And Then Comes the End* by David Ewert (Scottdale: Herald Press, 1980).

Glossary/Index

anti-Semitism   anti-Jewish attitudes and actions *(21, 27, 34, 83-84, 86, 91, 93-96, 105, 113, 122, 134, 142)*

aphikommen \ah´-fee-koh´-men\   (that which comes last)—broken piece of matzo served at end of Passover meal *(54-55)*

Ashkenazim \ahsch´-ken-ah´-zeem\   cultural Jewish group originating in Central and Eastern Europe which gave rise to most of the Jewish people in the world today; embraced Yiddish language *(68)*

bar mitzvah   (son of the law)—ceremony which welcomes a thirteen-year-old boy as an adult in the Jewish community *(75, 117, 121, 125, 129)*

bat mitzvah   (daughter of the law)—ceremony within Reform Judaism which recognizes the coming to adulthood of the thirteen-year-old girl *(75, 117)*

B. C. E., C. E.   (Before Common Era, Common Era)—designations used by Jewish people in place of B. C. (before Christ) and A. D. (Anno Domini—in the year of our Lord). One can use those designations (B. C. E., C. E.) in deference to the Jewish people. *(45, 72, 80, 101, 154-155)*

charoseth \ha-roh´-seth\   symbolic Passover food made of a mixture of chopped apples, nuts, raisins, cinnamon, and wine or grape juice; its reddish-brown color recalls the mortar the Israelite slaves used in building in Egypt *(53-54)*

Christian identity cults   contemporary white supremacist, racist groups which include the Jewish people as one of the groups they are prejudiced against; some would literally say that salvation is by race (the white race), not by grace; often express extreme anti-Semitism *(93)*

Conservative Judaism   the religious center of Judaism; a reaction to the more liberal Reform Jewish movement *(69-71)*

Crusades   Although these campaigns of the Middle Ages were organized by the European Roman church to "rescue" the "Holy Land" from the Muslims, they also brought terror and death to Jews who were persecuted and martyred by the Crusaders as they marched towards the Middle East, as well as in Jerusalem on at least one Crusade. *(21, 84, 88, 140)*

Felashas \fe-lah´-shas\   black Jewish people of Ethiopia *(68)*

Gemara \ge-mahr´-a\   commentary on the Mishnah *(71-72)*

Haggadah \ha-gah´-da\   printed order of Passover seder celebration *(53)*

Hanukkah   (dedication)—Late November or December festival which recalls the Jewish peoples' cleansing and rededicating of the temple after it had been defiled by the Syrian ruler Antiochus Epiphanes; a little consecrated oil miraculously lasted for eight days *(7, 35-36, 45-46)*

Hasidim \ha-see-deem´\   very Orthodox Jews with Ashkenazim roots who emphasize joyful emotions and mysticism *(68-69)*

Havdalah \hav-dah´-la\   (separation)—ceremony at sunset at end of the Sabbath, marking the beginning of the new week *(61, 121)*

Holocaust   systematic massacre of six million Jewish people during Hitler's regime in Nazi Germany at the time of World War II *(21, 71, 84, 92-93, 97)*

Inquisition   campaign in Spain and Portugal in the 15th century to rid the church of heretics; was especially vicious against Christianized Jewish people called Marranos (literally "swine") *(21, 84, 90, 140)*

kippah \kee-pah´\ Hebrew word for "skull cap" worn by Orthodox and Conservative Jewish men *(73)*

kosher \koh´-sher\ (fit)—refers to keeping the dietary laws of the Torah *(66, 74, 112, 117-118)*

Lubavitchers \loo-bah´-vitch-ers\ members of an Orthodox Jewish sect who are zealous Jewish missionaries and vehemently anti-Christian *(69)*

Maccabee \mack´-a-bee\, **Judah** leader of Jewish guerilla fighters who in 165 B. C. E. defeated the Syrians who were occupying Israel's land⁻ *(45)*

Maimonides \my-mon´-a-deez´\ (d. 1204)—Sephardic Jewish scholar who wrote down the thirteen principles of the Jewish faith *(68)*

matzo \mahtz´-a\ unleavened bread used at the time of the Passover festival *(26, 53-55, 89, 132)*

megillah \me-gil´-la\ special parchment scroll of the book of Esther; used in celebrating Purim *(51)*

Messianic Judaism Jewish movement which fully embraces Jesus (Yeshua) as the divine Son of God and the Messiah promised in the Hebrew Scriptures, while at the same time worshiping and living out faith in a distinctly Jewish style (practicing many of the Jewish traditions, those which do not conflict with faith in Yeshua) *(71, 77, 79, 112, 114, 118)*

mezuzah \me-zoo´-za\ tiny boxes containing portions of Scripture, attached to doorways of the Jewish home, to remind one of the constant presence of God and of his commandments *(74, 116)*

minyan \min´-yan\ number of men (ten) needed to hold a public worship service *(75)*

Mishnah \mish´-na\ commentary on the Torah by scholarly rabbis *(71-72)*

Nazarenes first Century Jewish movement which embraced faith in Jesus as the promised Messiah while maintaining their Jewish roots *(78-79)*

Orthodox Judaism the most traditional branch of the Jewish faith, insofar as practicing and keeping the Torah *(68-70)*

Passover (Pesach in Hebrew)—festival celebrating the "passing over" by the angel of death of those Jewish homes in Egypt which had blood of a lamb smeared above and on the sides of the door *(26, 36, 41, 49, 51-56, 62, 71, 89, 111, 155)*

pogroms terroristic and murderous attacks against Jewish people in Eastern Europe and Russia during the last several hundred years *(21, 91)*

Potok, Chaim \poh´-tak, keim\ contemporary Jewish writer and novelist *(67, 132)*

Protocols of the Elders of Zion a forged document of the late 19th century which presented the Jewish people as international conspirators; was popularized by people like Henry Ford and Gerald Winrod *(93)*

Purim \poo´-rim\ (lots, the casting of lots)—late winter festival remembering God's deliverance through Queen Esther's acts which helped rescue her people from the treacherous Haman *(36, 49-51, 86)*

Reconstructionism a small sub-group of Conservative Judaism which views God as a cosmic force rather than a personal being *(70)*

Reform Judaism a movement which has attempted to bring Jewish faith into the modern world; the ethics of the Jewish faith are emphasized more than traditional Jewish practices *(69-71)*

Rosh Hashanah \rohsh´-hah-shah´-nah\ (head of the year)—Jewish New Year festival held in the fall; also called Feast of Trumpets *(37-38, 46, 111)*

Sabbath (Shabbat in Hebrew, meaning "rest")—weekly festival for resting, worshiping God, and enjoying family *(7, 19, 36, 49, 57-62, 65-66, 70-71, 113, 115-116, 121)*

Samaritans mixed Jewish-Gentile group *(18, 68, 127)*

Schereschewski, Samuel Isaac \sher´-e-shoo´-ski\ Jewish believer (Episcopal priest) who did extensive Bible translation work in mainland China in the 19th century *(23)*

secular Jews those who are culturally Jewish but basically are unaffiliated with any of the Jewish religious groupings *(71)*

seder ceremonial family meal held Friday evening at the beginning of Sabbath; also the Passover meal *(26, 51-52, 54-55)*

Sephardim \se´-far-deem´\ cultural Jewish group dominant in Spain and the Mediterranean world in the Middle Ages; emphasized the arts and sciences *(68)*

Shavuot \sha´-voo-oht´\ (Hebrew name for Pentecost; means "weeks")—spring festival of firstfruits of the harvest; traditionally also refers to giving of the Law on Mt. Sinai; celebrated on fiftieth day after the firstfruits offering given just after Passover *(26, 32, 55-57, 115)*

Shema \she-mah´\ ("Hear!" in Hebrew)—the call to worship recited in Jewish services; "Hear, O Israel, the Lord our God, the Lord, is one" (Deuteronomy 6:4) *(74, 116, 143)*

shofar \shoh´-far\ ram's horn used as a trumpet to call people to attention *(36-37)*

Sukkot \sook-koht´\ ("tabernacles" in Hebrew; singular is sukkah)—refers to the Feast of Tabernacles, the fall festival which recalls the faithfulness of God to Israel in their wilderness wanderings between Egypt and Canaan *(41, 43-44, 46)*

synagogue a place of meeting for teaching, worship, and prayer, as well as for other gathered assemblies; the central focal point of the synagogue assembly room is the large cabinet which houses the scrolls of the Torah *(13, 16, 19, 47, 51, 61, 65-66, 70-72, 75-76, 78-79, 88, 111-113, 116, 121-122, 125, 131-132)*

tallit \tah´-leet\ prayer shawl worn by Orthodox and by some Conservative Jewish men *(73)*

Talmud \tahl´-mood\ consists of the Torah and the commentaries on the Torah (Mishnah and Gemara) *(66, 69, 71-72)*

tefillin \te-fill´-in\ phylacteries; small leather-covered boxes containing certain portions of Scripture worn on the forehead and the left arm by Torah-observant Jewish men when at worship *(73, 75)*

Tenach \te-nakh´\ acronym used to designate the Jewish Scriptures; the acronym is formed from "Torah" (the Law), "Neviim" (the Prophets), and "Ketuvim" (the Writings—Psalms, Proverbs, Chronicles, etc.) *(17, 71, 125, 139-140, 157)*

Torah \tour´-a or tohr´-a\ the five books of the Law (Genesis, Exodus, Leviticus, Numbers, Deuteronomy) but also used to refer to all 39 books of the Hebrew Scriptures *(43, 45, 65-66, 69-75)*

Torah-observant used to describe the more Orthodox Jewish people who keep the traditional Jewish practices *(65-66, 69, 76)*

"two-covenant theology"   erroneously states that the First Covenant (with Abraham and Moses) is sufficient today for Jewish people's salvation and that the New Covenant through Jesus is for Gentiles' salvation *(21)*

tzitzit \tsi´-tsit\   fringes of the tallit (prayer shawl) which are a reminder of the commandments of the Lord (see Numbers 15:37-41) *(73)*

yarmulke \yahr´-me-ka\   Yiddish word for "skull cap" worn by Orthodox and Conservative men *(73, 117)*

Yiddish   language embraced by the Ashkenazim; a mixture of Hebrew and German *(68, 73)*

Yom Kippur \yahm-kihp´-uhr or yohm´-kee-poor´\ (Day of Covering)—Day of Atonement, the one day of the year when the high priest entered the most holy place of the tabernacle or temple to sprinkle blood on the top of the ark of the covenant for the forgiveness of sin; today practicing Jewish people observe fasting and attend services in the synagogue to pray for forgiveness *(38-39, 41, 46, 106, 111)*

Zionism   movement begun by Theodore Herzl in the late 1800s to establish a homeland for the Jewish people *(94, 105-106)*

Calendar of Festival Dates

Year	5755 / 1994-95	5756 / 1995-96	5757 / 1996-97	5758 / 1997-98
ROSH HASHANAH	Sept. 6	Sept. 25	Sept. 14	Oct. 2
YOM KIPPUR	Sept. 15	Oct. 4	Sept. 23	Oct. 11
SUKKOT	Sept. 20	Oct. 9	Sept. 28	Oct. 16
HANUKKAH	Nov. 28	Dec. 18	Dec. 6	Dec. 24
PURIM	Mar. 16	Mar. 5	Mar. 23	Mar. 12
PASSOVER	Apr. 15	Apr. 4	Apr. 22	Apr. 11
SHAVUOT	June 4	May 24	June 11	May 31

Year	5759 / 1998-99	5760/1999-2000	5761 / 2000-01	5762 / 2001-02
ROSH HASHANAH	Sept. 21	Sept. 11	Sept. 30	Sept. 18
YOM KIPPUR	Sept. 30	Sept. 20	Oct. 9	Sept. 27
SUKKOT	Oct. 5	Sept. 25	Oct. 14	Oct. 2
HANUKKAH	Dec. 14	Dec. 4	Dec. 22	Dec. 10
PURIM	Mar. 2	Mar. 21	Mar. 9	Feb. 26
PASSOVER	Apr. 1	Apr. 20	Apr. 8	Mar. 28
SHAVUOT	May 21	June 9	May 28	May 17

James R. Leaman is pastor of Oxford Circle Mennonite Church, Philadelphia, Pennsylvania. He holds a Master of Divinity degree from Eastern Mennonite Seminary, a
Master of Arts in Pastoral Counseling from LaSalle University, is a member of Jewish Outreach Partnership in the
Philadelphia Area, and is chairperson of Shofar Committee
of Eastern Mennonite Board of Missions and Charities.
James is married to Beth (Kling) Leaman. They have two
children, Tim and Maria.